D0616084

THE
POWER
OF
POSITIVE
PARENTING

Dr. William Mitchell and Dr. Charles Paul Conn

Fleming H. Revell
A Division of Baker Book House Co
Grand Rapids, Michigan 49516

Front cover design by David Marty Design

To Carolyn, my partner in positive parenting and in life; our sons Billy and Michael, our daughter-in-law Janey, and our beautiful granddaughter, Carolyn Michelle Mitchell

H.W.M.

To my students at Lee College
and to their parents

C.P.C.

Contents

Foreword

Did you know that every thirty minutes, 29 children in the United States will attempt suicide? And that in the two hours it will take to read this book, the following will happen?
- –228 children will run away from home
- –56 teenage girls will give birth to illegitimate babies
- –88 girls under the age of nineteen will have an abortion
- –752 youngsters will experience a serious drinking problem
- –2740 teenagers will take some form of narcotics—all of them regular drug users

Each one of these self-destructive behaviors is *learned*—at home and in school. And the primary cause of all these behaviors is *negative attitudes and feelings of low self-esteem*. Drug use, alcoholism, irresponsible sexual behavior, illiteracy, and the high dropout rate from school and society are unmistakable signals of deep dissatisfaction.

In addition, over a million children each year suffer from emotional abuse. It is clear from the daily newspaper accounts of the tragedies epidemic in the lives of our youth that there are indeed crises with our nation's children and young people.

Dr. William Mitchell and Dr. Charles Paul Conn's nationally acclaimed book *The Power of Positive Students* focused on helping schools combat the causes of negative attitudes and low self-esteem. Now *The Power of Positive Parenting* addresses the home, the wellspring of the images we hold about ourselves and of the attitudes with which we will meet life's challenges.

Children's feelings about themselves are already well in place by the time they reach school age. A parent, the child's most powerful influence and primary example for learning in the home, can, on a continuing, day-by-day basis, learn and practice patterns of reinforcement to a child's positive feelings about himself. Success in a child's life is built from frequent successes; positive attitudes and behaviors reinforced in a systematic way help to build the sense of self-esteem that will redirect life's inevitable setbacks away from self-destructive behaviors.

The Power of Positive Parenting is a book for parents—to help mothers and fathers understand this ultimate human predicament. Dr. Mitchell and Dr. Conn have put together an outstanding program to help every home become risk-free—to become a place in which positive attitudes, self-worth, and success can be built, easily, painlessly, one step at a time.

—Denis E. Waitley, Ph.D.

Special Thanks

This book became a reality because of the encouragement and assistance from my secretary and friend, Mrs. Helen B. Dickerhoof. Also I would like to thank Ruth Baker and Charlotte Sigler for their help as well as being a sounding board.

H.W.M.

Grateful acknowledgment is made by the authors and WYNWOOD Press for permission to include the following:

IT'S OK, SON, EVERYBODY DOES IT—Reprinted from the Chicago Sun-Times, Inc., 1989.

From The Key to Your Child's Heart, by Gary Smalley (Word Books, 1984). Reprinted by permission of Word Incorporated, Dallas, Texas.

From The Language of Love, by Robert Fisher (Pathway Press, 1987). Reprinted by permission of Pathway Press, Cleveland, Tennessee.

Introduction

More than half of all learning takes place in the home. All parents want their children to be happy and succesful, but few parents understand the effect of positive attitudes on achieving these goals. *The Power of Positive Parenting* directs our attention to the home, the origin of our attitudes and skills, to address this problem.

The Power of Positive Parenting is a guide for parents from two of the nation's leading educators and authorities in attitude development, Drs. William Mitchell and Paul Conn. Drs. Mitchell and Conn explain—concisely and simply—the scientific base of attitude development and its importance in shaping children's behaviors in the home. *The Power of Positive Parenting* will lead you one step at a time in the development of more effective parenting skills. Specific suggestions, the "how to's" of developing positive attitudes and life skills, will help parents raise their children's self-esteem and learn to believe in themselves. It will also help them to develop high expectations for achievement and to learn to set and reach their goals in life.

Living a positive life will make an amazing difference in your children's lives—as well as your own. A positive life is there for anyone, you have only to begin. Begin with this book!

—Kenneth H. Blanchard

THE
POWER
OF
POSITIVE
PARENTING

1 Journey of Life— Make It a Success

Positive parenting—the teaching of positive attitudes—is the greatest gift one can give to a child.

Life is a trip. It has a definite beginning and ending, with a long, winding road connecting the two points. For most of us it is a long trip—seventy years or more, or over twenty-five thousand days. The quality of that journey depends more on the person making the trip than it does on the conditions or circumstances encountered along the way.

There are basically two kinds of people in the world, people with two different worldviews. The first group are those who believe that what they do makes very little difference, that life is so complex and the forces governing their happiness and success so powerful and so far beyond them that they must leave the outcome up to fate or luck. The second group holds a very different view. These people feel that what they do makes a critical difference in the outcome of their lives, that regardless of the roadblocks and obstacles along the way, they can set their own destination and follow their own road map. These people believe that "if it is to be, it's up to me."

I am a person who enthusiastically embraces the latter view. I believe that all of us, as individuals, can create the shape of our own tomorrows. The content of our attitudes and the tilt of our minds, not the particular set of circumstances that come our way, will determine whether or not our journey of life is a successful one.

I am also a religious person who believes in a personal and loving God. To some people, this may seem a peculiar combination—a strong belief in the power of the individual to determine his own future and yet a strong belief in the presence of an omnipotent God. But it should not seem a paradox at all. I am fully aware of the power of God to will whatever He chooses in my life, but I am equally aware that God leaves it up to me to live happily or miserably, depending on the way I respond to those conditions and circumstances beyond my control.

Only a foolish person would claim to control the events in his or her life. Life has no guarantees. The healthy person may be a paraplegic tomorrow; the wealthy man may be a pauper by the time the stock market closes; the happy mother may be grieving the loss of a child before the day ends. Life can be a tough journey on a rather indiscriminate basis, and only the most naive among us would forget that.

But there is a power far stronger than fate or circumstance—the extraordinary resilience and power of the God-given human spirit. I believe that the human spirit is the greatest natural force in the universe, the finest thing ever made by a creative God; and I believe that each of us can nurture and cultivate that human spirit within ourselves to bring about both a happy and a successful journey through life. It has enabled men and women in dozens of generations to rise singing from the graveside of a child; it has helped countless businessmen to rebuild great fortunes from the ashes of bankruptcy; it has made individuals in wheelchairs some of the most positive and productive people in our society. Further, I believe that parents who believe in the power of the human spirit to create a positive lifestyle can transmit that power to their children. This is the basic premise with which I begin.

I assume that all of us want the best for our children and are willing to make changes in our lives to provide the best for them. The changes I propose we make as parents are not changes in the schools our children attend, or in the neighborhoods in which we live, or even in the society that we have created for them. But the thing each of us can change is the way we think—the way we think about ourselves, about our human potential, and about our children.

I did not always understand the principles I share with you. In fact, fifty years ago, as a young boy, I may have been the most unlikely candidate you could imagine for teaching people how to believe in themselves. I suffered from low self-esteem and was one of the most negative, insecure children you would ever meet, and with what might appear to be good reason. I was small for my age, a poor boy growing up in a steel-mill town near Birmingham, Alabama. I was the product of what some people called in those days a "broken home," living with my mother and my grandmother in a time when divorce was much less common and more stigmatized than it is today.

A background of poverty, of course, need not be one that produces low self-esteem. There are many examples of homes in which money is scarce but positive emotional support is abundant, and a child's self-esteem not only can but does thrive in such homes. In my own case, however, both income and positive attitudes were in short supply.

The family from which I came placed little value on education; I was the first member of my family to be graduated from high school, much less go to college. Having a good job was as much as we hoped for from life; sometimes the men in our family had one, and sometimes they didn't.

I described my childhood at some length in *The Power of Positive Students*. Jobs were scarce and pay was low, and work in the steel mills was the only work we knew. We were poor, and so was everyone else we knew. Until I started school in the first grade, I had no way of knowing that in some homes there was enough food, clothing, and money to go around. The only big meals, those with meat on the table, came on Sunday afternoons, when our extended family would gather. The meat was almost always fried chicken, and in the Southern custom, we children ate after the adults were finished.

I learned to dread those family get-togethers because I was small for my age, extremely self-conscious about it, and painfully shy. After the meal it was our custom to congregate in the living room for music and singing. Those who could play the guitar did; those who could sing jostled for the stage. It seemed to me that everyone had a good time but me. I simply sought a corner and listened, always afraid that someone would drag me into the center of the room and reveal my lack of talent and self-confidence.

When I began school, I discovered for the first time that some people had more of almost everything than some others did. I became aware that I was from a poor family, from the wrong side of town. School lunches cost ten cents per day, but there was never any question about buying a hot lunch—we simply did not have the dime to spare. I carried my lunch from home—usually leftover biscuits from the breakfast table, occasionally with canned meat or fig preserves inside the biscuit—wrapped in a piece of newspaper. Those of us who were at the bottom of the lunchtime status ladder brought our food wrapped in newspaper. The significance of it was not lost on me, even as a seven- or eight-year-old. I was embarrassed to eat in the presence of other kids and would often toss my bundle of biscuits into the nearest trash can and spend the lunch period on the school playground.

As I grew, several important adults emerged to reshape, ever so gradually, my self-image. There was Mrs. McIndoe, my second-grade teacher. She saw me come into her classroom barefoot one cold winter morning. Taking great care to see that my classmates could not overhear us, she asked me where my shoes were and, when I told her I had none, made arrangements to take me that afternoon to the U.S. Steel Company commissary, where she bought new shoes for me. She managed to do this without doing further damage to my already tattered self-image; and throughout the school year, she worked at building my sense of self-esteem. She interceded at a critical time.

Thank God for sports, which in thousands of cases have given inferiority-stricken, lower-class kids like me a solid sense of self-worth for the first time in their lives. Throughout elementary and junior high school, athletics was my lifeboat; playing ball kept me afloat emotionally and psychologically. It gave me something to do that I could do well, and it brought me into contact with adults like Coach Minto, who further bolstered my self-confidence.

Coach Minto was the basketball coach at Rutledge Junior High. One afternoon, while I was playing basketball on the school's dirt playground after school, he singled me out and

told me, "I want you to try out for the varsity basketball team."
This was a stunning pronouncement to me. I would never
have dreamed of trying out for the varsity team; I was small,
and I was convinced I wasn't good enough. I would never
have voluntarily exposed myself to the possible rejection and
embarrassment of trying out. But he singled me out and
persuaded me to try.

Coach Minto was the first person who ever said to me, "You
can do it." He told me not to worry about my lack of height;
I was agile, quick, and aggressive. He was confident I could
help the team, and I played like a man possessed. Having
someone believe in me was like an addiction; I craved it and
I would have done anything for it.

When time came to leave junior high for the far more
intimidating West End High School, another adult entered my
sphere to teach me lessons in self-worth and personal achievement. This time it was not a coach but an ROTC instructor,
Sergeant Lacey, who took a scrappy mill-town kid in hand and
poured love and confidence into him. Sergeant Lacey made a
boxer out of me. He helped train kids for the local Golden
Gloves competition in Birmingham and talked me into taking
up the sport.

I entered the Golden Gloves, won many matches, and
eventually won the Birmingham championship in my weight
division. I got lots of local publicity and suddenly found
myself recognized by my peers. But, more important, I experienced once again the feelings of wanting to live up to someone's expectations and doing so. Sergeant Lacey believed in
me, and I measured up!

Soon after I won the Golden Gloves tournament, Sergeant
Lacey challenged me to get a date—my first—to the upcoming
ROTC ball. I had no car, no driver's license, had never had a
date before, and didn't know how to dance! "No problem,"

said Sergeant Lacey, "all that can be fixed. You borrow my car, I teach you how to drive and you get a license, you learn to dance, then asking a girl is easy." And that's the way it all worked out.

When the big night came, I dressed up in my ROTC uniform (I had never owned a suit or sport coat), got behind the wheel of Sergeant Lacey's Hudson, and felt ten feet tall!

With help from people like McIndoe, Minto, and Lacey, I was eventually graduated from high school, and after a two-year hitch in the army and working in the steel mill for a year, I entered college. By the time my schooling was over, I had earned not only a college degree, but a master's and a doctoral degree as well, and was such a committed believer in the power of education to change people's lives that I became a professional educator, first as a teacher and coach, later as a principal, and finally as a public school superintendent.

It was during my career as a superintendent that I first came to realize just how powerful the positive attitudes were that had been instilled in me by those significant adults. As an educator, I met thousands of young people who, like the young Bill Mitchell, were selling themselves short because no one had ever taught them how to live life positively.

When I first realized how vital positive thinking is in the journey through life, I decided to introduce it to an entire school district. The results were amazing, even to me.

2 Power of Positive Self— A Must for Success

People ask me why I am so committed to teaching positive self-worth to children. There are two answers.

The first is my own journey through childhood: I personally experienced the changes that occur when a child begins to believe in himself. But believing in something for oneself and believing that it can also work for others are two different things. In addition to my own life being changed by a positive self-image, I also saw its dramatic impact on an entire community in Sumter County, South Carolina.

I had gone to Sumter County as superintendent of the District Two school system. I had moved there in response to a challenge to manage a school system that had been described to me as one of the worst systems in the country. When I arrived in Sumter, I found that the system was as bad as advertised. Using almost every index by which public schools are measured, Sumter District Two was in trouble.

Sumter County is in central South Carolina. District Two covers a sparsely populated area of 676 square miles. The students, roughly ten thousand of them, were 60 percent black and 40 percent white. It was a rural district whose per capita income was well below the national average. At the time, about one fourth of the families were associated with Shaw Air Force Base, the area's leading employer.

I arrived in Sumter to find a school system in which none of its fifteen schools was accredited. Disciplinary suspensions had been so high that the district had been featured in a national journal article on student misbehavior. The military families assigned to Shaw Air Force Base had been highly vocal in their criticism of the school system, justifiably concerned about inadequate curriculum and facilities, poor student performance on national tests, improperly certified teachers, high levels of absenteeism, and chronic vandalism. Positive parental involvement was virtually nonexistent.

I battled these problems for four years, and a few of them *were* solved. New buildings were built, equipment was upgraded, and we made progress in several areas. But the more severe problems of poor student performance and low morale persisted; the overall climate of District Two failed to improve. Everyone seemed to realize that we still had a very poor school system and despaired of its ever getting much better. We were locked into a pattern of failure.

The fundamental problem in Sumter, which had not been affected by infusions of money and new buildings, was that most of the students thought of themselves as losers. They shared a deeply ingrained sense that they were inferior, and they performed accordingly. There was a sense of failure that pervaded the system, and it both issued from and contributed to an individual sense of failure that virtually every student experienced.

I was familiar with the concepts of Positive Mental Attitude (PMA) and self-esteem building but considered those concepts to have been designed for business and salesmanship rather than for public education. I had read many PMA-oriented motivational books and was aware that many analysts attributed the success of direct-sales businesses such as Amway, Tupperware, and various insurance companies to their heavy emphasis on mental attitude. But I wasn't a salesman, I was an educator, and before 1978 I had never seen the connection between those motivational uses of self-esteem principles and our problems in Sumter County.

The light finally dawned. I picked up a brochure advertising a motivational meeting in Chicago. A Board member and I attended, with an eye toward adapting what we heard to the educational dilemma of District Two. Once I realized how readily the whole literature and tradition of Positive Mental Attitude could be translated into educational applications, I came home feeling like a reborn administrator.

My staff and I began to develop a Positive Thinking program to sell Sumter County students on themselves. For the next two years, we used every means imaginable to convert our students into positive thinkers—champions in everything they might attempt:

- Billboards with short, upbeat messages appeared all over town.
- Every school day began with contemporary music on the school intercoms, songs with positive lyrics that conveyed the idea of self-worth.
- Teachers began their classes by reading brief "attitude boosters" to their students.

- Bumper stickers with positive slogans were distributed to students and parents.
- We conducted systemwide rallies featuring some of the nation's top motivational speakers, such as Norman Vincent Peale, Zig Ziglar, Olympic gold medalist Bob Richards, former Miss America Marilyn VanDerber, and William Raspberry, a columnist for the Washington *Post*.
- Laminated book covers, printed with positive attitude reminders, were given to students.
- Faculty and staff members, including nonteaching personnel such as custodians and cafeteria workers, attended special workshops designed to train them to communicate positive ideas to students.
- The day prior to achievement tests and other major exams, some of our schools conducted pep rallies, much like those held before important athletic events.
- Teachers were asked to make lists of negative words and expressions they used or heard others use and to supply positive substitutes for them.

In addition to these highly visible public activities, the heart of the program in District Two was the hard work of our teachers, day in and day out, in implementing Positive Thinking concepts in their instruction, grading, and classroom management. They did this in dozens of small ways, and it was these efforts, the backbone of the Positive Thinking program, that began to build the self-worth of students and employees.

The success of the Positive Thinking program proved far beyond our highest expectations. Over the next two years we not only witnessed but *measured* dramatic gains in almost every category by which the effectiveness of schools can be evaluated:

- Grades, as well as performance on state and national standardized exams, improved throughout the system.
- Reading scores by elementary students jumped phenomenally,

with the number of third-graders performing above the national average increasing from 10 percent to 49 percent in one school.

- Absenteeism dropped sharply.
- Discipline problems decreased in almost every high school and junior high school in the system.
- Vandalism, such a major problem in previous years (window-glass breakage alone had cost the system $30,000 a year), became practically nonexistent.
- Participation increased in extracurricular activities such as band and chorus.
- Disciplinary suspensions dropped from 450 students per month to 70 per month.
- Referrals for both drug and alcohol abuse in secondary schools decreased.
- Athletic teams won regional and state championships for the first time in their history.

The cure for District Two's malaise had turned out to be a dose of old-fashioned positive thinking!

After the extraordinary success of the Positive Thinking program in Sumter District Two, I was eager to test the applicability of the concept in another place. I accepted the position of superintendent of schools in Allegany County, Maryland, a school system with very different demographics from Sumter District Two. There, as in my previous school district, the program proved highly successful. It became known as The Power of Positive Students, commonly referred to as POPS.

The POPS Program began to attract national attention. At the urging of many leaders in the educational and business community, I decided to leave school administration to head up a nationwide, nonprofit foundation whose mission would be to introduce this program in school systems and homes around the country.

The POPS Foundation is now hard at work and has implemented our version of self-esteem training in each of the fifty states and in many foreign countries. In school after school, large and small, urban and rural, with all sorts of constituencies, the outcome has been the same—students who feel good about themselves work harder, avoid trouble, and perform better than those who do not.

My reflections on the experience, recorded in *The Power of Positive Students*, are still valid today. It was as if we had turned loose in our community a force that was far more potent than we had imagined, and even the most optimistic among us were startled by the results. By bringing about even small improvements in our students' view of themselves, we received enormous payoffs in their performance.

The impact of that experience did more than make me a better educator. It made me a better father and a better husband; it taught me things about children that I hadn't learned in all my years in graduate school. It helped me understand why things had worked out as they had in my own life and how my experience could be used to help others.

Sometimes I wish that I could retrieve my earlier days as a father and live them over again, knowing what I now know about a child's self-esteem and how to build it. I would be a better father to my two little boys if I had it to do over again, not because I would love them more or because I would try harder, but because I understand so much better how important it is to be a father who instills in his children self-esteem and self-confidence.

I have become increasingly impressed with the importance of positive parenting in the development of a child. As a professional educator I was naturally trained to analyze a child's behavior in terms of what he or she gains or does not gain in the *school* setting, and I remain a strong advocate of the importance of positive schools and positive teachers. Our country needs them, our children need them, and I have devoted my professional life to that goal.

It is clear to me, however, that by the time children reach kindergarten, much of their self-image is already firmly in place. Even if every school were an oasis of positive affirmation for every child, it still could not undo the lessons about self-worth that have already been instilled at home.

Any elementary school teacher will testify that students come with widely varying attitudes about their value as persons. At best, the teacher is engaged in remedial work with many of the students' attitudes. Because the parent, not the teacher, is the primary source of the child's sense of who and what he is, additional substantial amounts of parental involvement are needed for the job of self-esteem training. Parents form the natural first line of support for the child; more than anyone else in the child's life, they are in a position to teach children how to create their own tomorrows.

The problem parents face is that unlike teachers, they come to the task with no specific training in child psychology or in the principles of self-esteem development. Most approach the challenge of parenting equipped with a great love for the child, a desire to rear the child as well as possible, and only an intuitive notion of how to go about it. Fortunately, the parental instincts are usually reasonably sound ones, and most mothers and fathers turn out to be good parents in spite of themselves. But the principles of positive thinking, so potent when applied in the educational setting, have just as much relevance when applied in the home, with potentially far greater impact. In all the many relationships of human life, it is difficult to imagine a more powerful figure than that of a positive parent.

3 Preparation—Key to Success

If life is a journey, then we obviously must make certain preparations if we expect to travel it successfully. All of us understand that in our professional career goals; we would not expect to build a successful medical practice without preparing ourselves in medical school, or to make a fortune in the stock market without the preparation of learning the difference between a margin call and an option!

But in the most important task of our lives, that of parenting, we sometimes assume that we need no particular preparation. We expect to marry, have babies, and somehow become instinctively skillful parents. Unfortunately, this is not the case. Effective parents are those who understand that preparation is the key to success.

31

The journey of life is similar to a daily exercise program. It is a step-by-step conditioning routine, a routine of preparing for, working toward, and attaining higher and higher goals of physical and emotional fitness.

Among the millions of people who jog, there are those who prepare for it properly and those who do not. For the jogger, preparation begins with the selection of the proper shoes, and then stretching and bending exercises to avoid unnecessary strain and tear on the muscles. Next, the jogger must set an initial goal—a block, a mile, or a marathon. At the outset, he must realize that he will contend with various discomforts: heat, injury, uneven surfaces. Once the jogger sets his mind to overcoming these discomforts, he will achieve his goal more quickly. In doing so, he will experience the emotional reward of attaining his goal, and the physical reward of a stronger body.

Our day-to-day lives are absolutely chock-full of obstacles, including financial strain, illness, and frustrations with our job, family, and friends. Without proper preparation, we have greater difficulty overcoming these problems and attaining happiness and success.

We must *prepare* for unexpected problems that lie ahead because we will certainly experience at least some of them. Dr. Norman Vincent Peale once said to me, as we were driving to one of his speaking engagements, "Billy, as long as you live, you will always have problems. They won't be the same problems; they will change. So you must expect them, and learn to solve them and use them as stepping-stones to success."

Failure to accept and solve setbacks is the curse of emotional well-being. As I travel on my own journey of life, I find people who seem to be born winners—yet, they stumble continuously and will probably never achieve success or reach their potential. Why? Because they are unable to cope successfully with adversities or maladies in their lives. On the other hand, I have seen others who were given little chance to succeed go on to accomplish great things. They did so because they were able to cope with their problems in a positive way.

Having spent the major part of my life as an educator, I am familiar with tragedies resulting at least partially from academic failure. I knew a bright young girl who had set her sights on making the National Honor Society; it was virtually an obsession. And despite working long and hard to attain this goal, she barely missed being named. It marked a turning point in her life. So fragile was her ego that she began neglecting her studies, she allied herself with an undesirable element of her peers, abandoned plans for college, eventually bore a child out of wedlock, and had a brief, disastrous marriage. At the age of twenty she became a suicide statistic.

I have seen comparable tragedies in the business world — lives wasted when anticipated promotions did not materialize, a broken marriage following a disillusioned businessman's dependence on alcohol. All are examples of persons unprepared for setbacks.

Personal, business, and professional failures are similar to the beginning jogger who never attains his initial goal. The reason is that he doesn't truly work at it and lacks the mental toughness and determination to shrug off setbacks. In short, most of the people who fail simply did not adequately prepare themselves to overcome obstacles on their journey of life.

General Douglas MacArthur once said, "Preparation is the key to success." There is no higher calling than parenthood, and perhaps no higher aspiration than that of being a positive parent. When one brings a child into the world, the task of parenting must be seen as a challenge. Smart parents, though

they are not intimidated by the task, are nevertheless more
keenly aware that it will require their very best effort.

Let me share with you the following "open letter to parents"; it clearly shows the magnitude of the challenge that awaits every new parent:

Dear Mom and Dad,
　　If you really love me, then please . . .

DON'T SPOIL ME. I know that I should not have all
that I ask for; I'm only testing you.

DON'T BE AFRAID TO BE FIRM WITH ME. I prefer
it. It makes me feel more secure.

DON'T LET ME FORM BAD HABITS. I have to rely
on you to detect them in the early stages.

DON'T MAKE ME FEEL SMALLER THAN I AM. It
only makes me behave stupidly "big."

DON'T CORRECT ME IN FRONT OF PEOPLE IF
YOU CAN HELP IT. I'll be much more receptive if you
talk quietly with me in private.

DON'T ALWAYS PROTECT ME FROM CONSE-
QUENCES. Sometimes I need to learn the hard way.

DON'T NAG. If you do, I will protect myself by
ignoring you.

DON'T MAKE RASH PROMISES. Remember that I
feel let down when promises are broken.

DON'T FORGET THAT I CANNOT ALWAYS EX-
PLAIN MYSELF AS WELL AS I WOULD LIKE. My answers can't always satisfy you.

DON'T BE INCONSISTENT. That completely confuses me and makes me lose faith in you.

DON'T PUT ME OFF WHEN I ASK QUESTIONS. If you do, you will find that I stop asking and seek information elsewhere.

DON'T TELL ME MY FEARS ARE SILLY. They are terribly real to me, and you can reassure me if you try to understand.

DON'T SUGGEST THAT YOU ARE PERFECT OR INFALLIBLE. It's too great a shock when I discover that you are neither.

DON'T FORGET I LOVE EXPLORING. I couldn't learn without it, so please put up with it.

DON'T FORGET HOW QUICKLY I AM GROWING UP. It must be very difficult for you to remember that, but please try.

DON'T FORGET THAT I CAN'T THRIVE WITHOUT LOTS OF UNDERSTANDING AND LOVE, BUT I DON'T NEED TO TELL YOU THAT, DO I?

Love,

Your Child

This poignant letter underscores just how multifaceted the role of the parent is, and how sensitive and fragile the spirit of the young, growing child can be. For young men and women approaching or entering parenthood for the first time, the journey of parenting sometimes seems like walking through a minefield: one must keep moving ahead, but any step may bring disaster. We become painfully aware that being a parent is something they never taught us how to do in school. It is our most demanding adult role, the results of which will be longest lasting, and yet it is the very role for which no curriculum is able to prepare us.

Preparation for parenting, then, is like preparation for life. It is primarily a matter of attitudinal and emotional preparation. The only meaningful way to get ready for being a mother or father is to develop the positive mental and emotional habits that produce happy and effective children.

The news of impending childbirth usually sends Mom and Dad into a slew of material and superficial preparations, especially if the child is the firstborn. We rush out to decorate the nursery, begin shopping for baby clothes, start reading articles on the advantages of breast-feeding versus the bottle, and begin stocking up on baby food. Dad starts noticing roller skates in toy-store windows and begins to worry about the high cost of college tuition.

But the most important type of preparation is not to buy books on how to choose the perfect diaper, or even to pick up early learning tips from "Sesame Street." The best preparation for parenting is to begin paying attention to one's own habits of thought and attitude and to commit to the kind of relentless optimism and positive mind-set that will communicate to the child, in a million small ways, that he is a person of worth and importance and that the world into which he was born is filled with hope and promise.

The most important qualities in a good parent have nothing to do with the ability to provide state-of-the-art toys or having a Ph.D. in child psychology. The qualities of good parenting do not depend on income level or educational status. They are within the reach of every caring individual.

PATIENCE in parents builds a strong heart. It shapes and molds the young child from the start.

ACCEPTANCE in parents prompts feelings of comfort and security.

RESPECT in parents evokes courtesy and admiration, and stimulates the child to regard others with consideration.

ENCOURAGEMENT in parents paves the way to inspiring the child's best in each day.

NOBILITY in parents develops worthiness and dignity. It generates in the child self-esteem and ability.

TRUTHFULNESS in parents forms the roots of honesty and creates in the young child a desire for sincerity.

Are you preparing for parenthood by developing those six important qualities? If you are, that is a more significant kind of preparation than anything else you might do.

4 Ethical Behavior— Foundation for Success

One aspect of positive parenting most frequently overlooked is the importance of giving children a foundation in ethical and moral principles.

I refer not to religious faith as such—though most ethical principles issue from spiritual values of some sort—but rather to a set of basic moral principles that are shared by virtually all religions. As a bare minimum, ethical standards are the basis on which an orderly life is built, and it is the responsibility of parents to transmit these values to their children.

Here is a list of the kinds of values to which I refer:

fairness	preparedness
cooperation	courtesy
compassion	loyalty

self-control	dedication
determination	conviction
conscientiousness	generosity
integrity	kindness
responsibility	helpfulness
promptness	honor
reliability	justice
honesty	tolerance
courage	truthfulness

These are rather broad categories of behavior, and some may be better described as personality characteristics rather than as ethical values per se, but the list gives an idea of the kinds of values that are the ethical and moral foundation on which civilized human interaction depends. Persons who have not learned these values have great difficulty on the journey through life.

The current generation of young people has seen the rapid erosion of society's ethical and moral foundation. It seems that as many newspaper headlines tell of human moral failure as of natural disasters or political maneuvers. Ethical breakdown is one of the diseases of our current culture.

Consider these news stories:

- Marine guards at the American Embassy in Moscow willingly open the doors to KGB agents.
- An FBI agent is arrested for spying—the first such case in the history of the FBI.
- A television evangelist is forced to resign from his ministry after admitting to an extramarital sexual tryst and paying "hush money" to keep the secret.
- A university is required to dismantle its football program for one year after being found guilty of repeatedly breaking the rules surrounding the recruitment of players.
- Several successful stockbrokers on Wall Street are indicted for illegally making large profits from insider information.

- A Democratic presidential candidate abandons his campaign after disclosure of an extramarital relationship.
- The Reagan administration is rocked by the news of a covert operation conducted from within the White House to sell arms secretly to Iran and divert the profits to Nicaraguan "contra" rebels, all in apparent violation of the law.

Such scandals have become so common, and touch such a wide variety of sectors of our society, that most of us agree that the breakdown of moral values is becoming a national problem. The learning of ethical standards begins at home. The child's first tendency toward a sense of right and wrong comes in the subtle, almost imperceptible signals he receives while still very young, long before reaching the age of rational thought about morality.

Parents who wish to give their children a head start toward developing a strong moral code can observe these common-sense guidelines:

1. *Create a home environment of justice and fairness.*

Justice and fair play are the core values of most ethical principles. One of the leading theorists in moral development has said that the single most eloquent statement of morality in human history was the familiar "Golden Rule" from the Bible: "Do unto others as you would have them do unto you." It is possible to develop a home environment in which this kind of reciprocal just treatment is the norm.

Catherine Stonehouse, a specialist in early childhood ethical development, says, in her book *Patterns in Moral Development:*

> The atmosphere or environment teaches more subtly than the planned curriculum, but the impact of the unplanned

curriculum may have a deeper, more lasting influence. Those who are concerned about moral development will want to give careful attention to the unplanned curriculum—that is, the atmosphere and environment in which the child is developing.

In the study of moral development it has been noted that the kind of environment in which a child lives influences his progress in development. For example, a person's understanding of what is fair or just will develop if he is part of a family and a class which treats persons fairly. If the child does not experience justice he may never come to fully understand what justice is.

One of the most important things an adult can do to help the child develop morally is to provide him with the kind of atmosphere that facilitates moral development. Several characteristics are essential to a healthy environment of moral development: mutual respect, a sense of belonging, justice, and openness.

2. *Set a parental example that exhibits a high ethical standard.*

The single most powerful teaching tool is parental example, and this is perhaps truer in the moral area than in any other. A parent who consistently breaks the rules but lectures his child to do otherwise is teaching with his example much more powerfully than with his lectures. The old cliché "Do as I say, not as I do" is testimony to the prevalent problem of parental behavior not matching up to parental preachings.

The following anecdote is extracted from an article in the Chicago *Sun-Times:*

IT'S OK, SON, EVERYBODY DOES IT

When Johnny was six years old, he was with his father when they were caught speeding. His father handed the officer a twenty-dollar bill with his driver's license. "It's OK, son," his father said as they drove off. "Everybody does it."

When he was eight, he was at a family council presided over by Uncle George, on the surest means to shave points off the income tax return. "It's OK, kid," his uncle said. "Everybody does it."

When he was nine, his mother took him to his first theater production. The box office man couldn't find seats until his mother discovered an extra five dollars in her purse. "It's OK, son," she said. "Everybody does it."

When he was twelve, he broke his glasses on the way to school. His Aunt Francine persuaded the insurance company that they had been stolen, and they collected seventy-five dollars. "It's OK, kid," she said. "Everybody does it."

When he was fifteen, he made right guard on the high school football team. His coach showed him how to block and, at the same time, grab the opposing end by the shirt so the official couldn't see it. "It's OK, kid," the coach said. "Everybody does it."

When he was sixteen, he took his first summer job at the supermarket. His assignment was to put the overripe strawberries in the bottom of the boxes and the good ones on top where they would show. "It's OK, kid," the manager said. "Everybody does it."

When he was eighteen, Johnny and a neighbor applied for a college scholarship. Johnny was a marginal student. His neighbor was in the upper three percent of his class, but he couldn't play right guard. Johnny got the scholarship. "It's OK, son," his parents said. "Everybody does it."

When he was nineteen, he was approached by an upperclassman who offered the test answers for fifty dollars. "It's OK, kid," he said. "Everybody does it."

Johnny was caught and sent home in disgrace. "How could you do this to your mother and me?" his father said. "You

never learned anything like this at home." His aunt and uncle
were also shocked.

If there's one thing the adult world can't stand, it's a kid who
cheats. . . .

3. *Discuss the ethical implications of everyday decisions with
your children.*

Children need to learn to ask "Why?" in regard to rules and
ethical decisions. It is not good enough merely to insist on
justice and fair play in the home, or even solely to set a high
ethical example; the child should be taught the *reasons* for
behaving ethically and with a regard for rules.

Morality is in large part a cognitive experience. It develops
as the child develops intellectually and is able to think about
what his behavior means in respect to the rights and concerns
of other people. To illustrate this point, a small infant certainly
does not behave in an ethical manner. He grabs whatever he
wants, behaves however he likes, and generally operates in a
fashion that takes into account nobody but himself. Is this
because babies are inherently unethical? Of course not. It is
because infants are not intellectually advanced enough to
understand a code of ethics, and such intellectual growth is a
prerequisite for true moral development.

Sometimes the most conscientious parents, or the strictest
parents, fail to take time to explain to their children *why* certain
behaviors are acceptable or unacceptable. Their children consequently grow up with a very keen understanding of au-
thority but little commitment to ethical behavior on their own.
Parents should constantly help their children to relate the
abstract principles of fair play to the specific behaviors that
correspond to those principles.

Why do we pay for the newspaper instead of stealing it from
the sidewalk paper rack? Not to avoid getting caught; not

merely because it is against the law; but because to steal the paper would be an abuse of another person who rightly owns the paper and must sell it to get a fair return on his work. That is the kind of explanation about ethical decisions that helps children make the connective link between principles and behavior.

5 Attitude—Invisible Heartbeat of Success

W. Clement Stone, founder and president of Combined Insurance Company of America, said, "There is a little difference in people, but that little difference makes a big difference. The little difference is attitude and the big difference is whether it is positive or negative."

Attitudes cannot be seen, heard, smelled, or tasted but we can be absolutely certain of their presence and their capacity to assist or hinder us in attaining our goals. Attitudes are the very heartbeat of success—invisible, yes, but one can be sure that within the heart of every successful person there constantly beat positive attitudes.

Though attitudes are invisible, their manifestations can be observed in an individual's facial expressions, tone of voice, or body language in various situations. These attitudes are more important to success than skills or knowledge, and they often make the difference between success and failure.

Exactly what is an attitude? Simply this: it is a habit. An attitude is a mental or emotional habit, a state of mind. It is a disposition to act or react in a given manner. Negative attitudes, or bad mental habits, lead to failure. Positive attitudes, or good habits of the mind, are the invisible heartbeat of success.

As a former football coach, as well as an exponent of positive thinking, I followed the exploits of Vince Lombardi and the Green Bay Packers with something approaching awe. Not because of his game strategy—his playbook was not particularly complicated: his offense was based on simple fundamentals of blocking, tackling, and timing, with eleven men executing in flawless unison—but because of his mental approach to coaching. Just as General George Patton was a master of mental toughness in preparing for war, so Vince Lombardi was a genius in instilling the "I can, I will" attitude in the minds of his players.

Lombardi joined the Packers in 1959 as head coach and general manager, coaching thereafter for eight seasons. Prior to Lombardi's arrival, the Packers had been the league's worst doormat for years. They were a ragtag bunch, a waste of basically good talent, uninspired, torn by lack of self-respect stemming from negative attitudes. In their minds, it was not a question of whether they would lose an upcoming game, but only by how many points!

In his first press conference as head coach, Vince Lombardi proclaimed, "Gentlemen, I have never been associated with a loser—and I don't intend to start now!" In the days that followed, he set out to reverse his players' bad emotional habits. He was tough, but he was fair. Players who violated his rules were tongue-lashed at best, and in some cases traded away. One All-Pro Packer offensive lineman was reportedly asked if Lombardi treated all his players alike. "Sure," he answered, "he treats us all alike—like dogs!"

But in that first season, under their iron-willed new coach, the Green Bay Packers finished with a winning record, their first in a decade. Lombardi taught them to be winners; he reversed their bad habits, leading them to the water and letting them taste success.

It was not surprising, then, that in their most memorable game, the 1967 championship game against the Dallas Cowboys, the Packers came from behind in almost unbelievable circumstances to win. With sixteen seconds to go, and the ball on the Cowboy one-yard line, the Packers needed a touchdown to win it all.

It was a time to show their mental toughness, or to fold. They rose to the challenge and scored the touchdown that won the most memorable playoff game in pro football history. So what if the temperature was twelve degrees below zero? So what if the chill factor was thirty-three below? So what if the heating elements under the field had broken and left the turf a frozen pond, making it virtually impossible for offensive linemen to get the footing necessary for good blocking.

The Packers got the job done that day because they had been taught to believe in themselves. Although physically numbed by the cold, they exhibited the positive mental attitudes of success which had been so deeply instilled in them and which made them great champions, season after season. The point is this: because attitudes are habits, and because habits are formed through repetition, attitudes can be changed! They can be permanently altered through a change in one's thought processes.

According to research, 85 percent of success in life derives from attitudes rather than from intelligence or innate ability. It is also true that one's initial attitudes are formed no later than age nine or ten, and most of them even earlier. It is far easier to formulate the correct attitudes early in life than to change them in adulthood. And that simple fact alone makes the responsibility of the parent loom even larger. *Positive parenting—the teaching of positive attitudes—is the greatest gift one can give to a child.*

Here are some things you might do to help your child acquire a positive attitude:

1. *Conditioning*

You suggest positive and negative thoughts to your children every day. Make certain that the messages you send, both verbally and nonverbally, are positive. "Thank you for helping, Billy" or "That was an excellent idea, Jane"—positive messages. Nonverbal expressions of approval can be conveyed by a loving touch, pleasant expressions, a hug, or a wink of approval.

2. *Role Model*

Set the example. Be a positive role model. Let your children know that you work hard to have a positive attitude and feel good about yourself. Look for the good in everything that happens. For example, suppose you run out of gas while on vacation. While you are waiting for gas, use the time to take pictures of the countryside or city buildings that are around. You are helping children to learn to look for the best in every situation.

3. *Reinforcement*

Use positive reinforcement frequently. "Catch your children doing things right" and reward them. For example, when children have chores to perform such as carrying out trash or making their beds, and they perform the chores without being reminded to do so, don't overlook the accomplishment. Express your pleasure at their having completed their chores. Give praise, recognition, a special privilege, or increased responsibility for doing a good job. Constantly emphasize the good things they do instead of the bad.

4. *Climate*

Provide a positive climate in your home. The physical setting of your home is one aspect of a positive climate. Make your home attractive, comfortable, and orderly. Interaction between family members is another aspect of a positive climate. Expressions of caring, loving, and concern let each person know that he or she is valued, accepted, trusted, and respected.

5. *Multimedia*

Encourage the reading of quality literature. Read to your children frequently, and provide informative books for them to read. Help children select television and radio programs that are informative, entertaining, and appropriate for their age. Provide opportunities for such things as listening to quality music, attending art galleries and museums, and seeing dramatic presentations.

6. *Support*

Show interest in your children's world. Join the P.T.A., visit their school, help with their homework, attend special school activities. Your interest and support will help to foster a positive attitude.

7. *Responsibility*

Give your children responsibility so they will feel important and valued. Demonstrate your confidence in them by giving them tasks they can carry out successfully. The tasks must be appropriate to the age level of the child. For example, a child may have the responsibility of making his bed each morning. Don't expect a five-year-old to make a bed as tidily as a twelve-year-old, but the important thing is to expect each child to do his best, and for him to know that you hold him accountable for the completion of the chore.

8. *Birds of a Feather*

Provide opportunities for your children to be in the presence of others, both peers and adults, who have positive attitudes. Association is important because of the influence that modeling can have toward building a positive outlook. You are known by the company you keep.

9. *Self-Talk*

Helping children learn to use positive self-talk is a vitally important skill in building positive attitudes. Teach children to take time as they prepare for their day to suggest to themselves such thoughts as, "I've really studied my spelling, and I'm going to get a good grade." At the end of the day, recap good things that have happened. Planned use of positive self-talk in the morning and at night develops the habit of spontaneous use of positive self-talk throughout the day.

As a parent interested in the development of a positive child, you must be both student and teacher. You already have an ingrained set of attitudes, some of which are good and others of which need to be changed.

The teacher part of you must decide what constitutes good and bad habits. This can be done by observing your friends, co-workers, and other acquaintances. Note which ones you consider highly successful, moderately successful, or unsuccessful or stalemated in life. Evaluate their personalities, their lifestyles, their habits, and make a mental list of which of their characteristics reflect *positive* attitudes and which reflect *negative* attitudes.

Next, objectively analyze yourself. Determine your strong and weak points. Dwell on your positive assets and decide to strengthen your areas of weakness.

The next step is for you as the student to make a commitment to self-improvement. You must recognize that your attitudes are a result of personal habits, and pledge yourself to constant self-discipline, determination, and persistence in reversing those attitudes you recognize as negative.

As your own teacher, convince yourself that your mind is nothing more than a computer. It is constantly being programmed. It is given instructions from dozens of sources— from people you meet, from the print and broadcast media, and from many other types of conscious and unconscious stimuli.

Guarding one's mind from the input of destructive material requires constant attention. It can be done by avoiding movies and television shows with themes of despair or violence, and by choosing magazines and books which elevate positive role models rather than negative ones. Ordinary conversations must be monitored, to prevent drifting into the habit of playing "ain't it awful" as our typical conversational tone. Another way of controlling input is by identifying those individuals who are always negative, rancorous and bitter, and spending as little time with them as possible. When we spend most of our time around people who are mostly negative thinkers and talkers, we cannot help but ingest their sour attitudes to some extent.

With that in mind, take responsibility for the fact that *you* are the chief programmer of your own mind. By controlling what is fed into your brain, you can control what comes out in the form of behaviors and their consequences.

You must promise yourself that you will admit only positive stimuli and counteract negative stimuli. Thus, by controlling the input to your personal computer you will govern its output.

Input determines output. A cliché of the computer world is "garbage in, garbage out," which means that if one feeds bad information into a computer, the computer will always give bad conclusions back. I once heard Pat Boone remark, "You cannot put garbage into a well and not eventually pollute the water." This is true with our minds. You cannot continuously put negative thoughts into the mind and not expect to experience negative consequences in your life. Garbage in, garbage out.

When positively programmed, however, the mind will respond to adversity with a bright outlook. To illustrate this point, I enjoy telling a story of two shoe salesmen who had very different attitudes. Both were sent to a newly discovered Pacific island inhabited by primitive natives. On arriving, Salesman A called his home office and exclaimed: "Hey boss, send the company plane down here right away and get me out of this place! There is no shoe business here; the natives are running around *barefoot!*"

Salesman B, on the other hand, was a true positive thinker. He too called his home office, but with a radically different message: "Hey boss, I found us a bonanza! Rush me all the shoes you can—all sizes, all styles, all colors. These poor natives are running around *barefoot!*"

The difference between Salesman A and Salesman B was the little difference in outlook that makes a big difference.

William James, the father of modern American psychology, said that the most important discovery of our time is that we can alter our lives by altering our attitudes. Once we learn that lesson for ourselves, we can teach it to our children, and the resulting changes in their behavior will change the consequences of their lives.

The greatest lesson I ever learned about the difference attitude can make for a kid was taught me by a youngster at West End High School in Birmingham, when I was coaching there. The boy's name was Bill Battle. At the age of thirteen, he was five feet five inches tall and about 160 pounds. As a candidate for the football team, he was an outright misfit. The coaches didn't even want to give him a uniform, but he insisted that he wanted to play football.

The first year Billy was moved from one position to another. No one found a niche for him, so he wound up as a human blocking dummy. But through it all, this gutsy kid never missed practice, and he never complained. He always gave his best, although that was usually not very good.

The second year, things got no better for Bill. He was shifted from tackle, to center, to end, and never got a chance to play in a game. But he never gave up; he still insisted that he would be a football player.

As a junior, he grew to about five-foot-eight and 175 pounds, but he still was just a chunky kid who loved football and never missed practice, and who impressed his teammates and all of us coaches with his unfailing optimism and positive attitude. He was so slow that his teammates called him Turtle; they liked him, and used the nickname affectionately, and he seemed not to mind. They would stand on the goal line and chant "Turtle! Turtle!" to him as he huffed and puffed his way through the wind sprints that usually concluded our practices.

In the middle of his junior year, Bill was put into a game unexpectedly, because we literally ran out of available players for the defensive end position. To everyone's amazement, he not only played well, he played brilliantly, and a Birmingham newspaper named him Player of the Week! He continued to play—not spectacularly, but well—until the end of the season.

That chance to play seemed to unlock in Bill Battle an enormous reserve of commitment and energy. That summer he went on a weight program. He gave up baseball to begin running, and to concentrate on the upcoming football season. He set high senior-year goals for himself and totally committed himself to becoming an outstanding football player.

Bill's body cooperated with him; a growth spurt, combined with his weight program, brought him back for the senior year at six feet two inches, and 180 pounds. He was a great-looking physical specimen. It was hard to remember why he had ever been called Turtle. That year he became one of the best high school football players ever to strap on a helmet; he made All-City, All-State, and All-American. He then accepted a scholarship with the University of Alabama and was part of a national championship team, playing in three major bowl games. At the age of twenty-eight, he became the head football coach at the University of Tennessee—the youngest head coach of a major college team in the country!

Bill Battle had the attitude of a champion. He refused to let negative predictions, comments, or ideas damage his desire to become an outstanding football player. Eventually, it was that attitude that proved to be more powerful than the natural skills and talents of any of his teammates. It took him to the top.

ATTITUDE ACTIVITY

I can if I think I can!

Each week, have your child positively state a task that he/she wants to accomplish. For example, "I, Marcy, will get at least seven out of ten spelling words correct." Have your child make the statement verbally and in writing before he/she leaves for the day. REMEMBER to encourage the attitude, "I am a winner for trying!"

6 Belief in Self—Cornerstone of Success

Jesus Christ, the greatest teacher who ever lived, changed human life, partly because He lifted people up and dwelt on their strengths and not on their weaknesses. His personal philosophy included these words: "All things are possible to him who believes."

The single most important attitude affecting human performance is belief in oneself. When people believe in themselves good things start happening. Belief is the motivating force that enables some to achieve. Each of us often needs another person to say to us, "I believe in you; you can do it." But the sustaining, ever-present ability a person possesses to say that to himself can be even more powerful.

Self-belief is the basic factor in attaining success. It is the thermostat that regulates what we accomplish in life. If you believe you are the best, you will soon act like the best, and then you will become the best.

The wife of a friend of mine, a woman in her early fifties, learned to drive an automobile as a teenager. Like many others, she had enormous difficulty coordinating her hands and feet in shifting gears. While she was still learning to drive, she began dating my friend, who had a car with automatic transmission. With his car she soon passed her driver's test. To this day, however, she is convinced that she is incapable of learning to drive a car with a stick shift, and rather than tell herself she can and will learn, she is content to sit home whenever her car, the only automatic in the family, is in the shop for service. And this is a woman who rips through crossword puzzles with a pen! This is a woman who beats her entire family at Trivial Pursuit! This is a woman who was offered the position of office manager in a regional branch of one of the nation's top corporations!

Self-belief is a state of mind, an attitude, a habit that can be developed. One should not confuse belief, however, with impractical wishful thinking. (It would be futile, for example, for one who had lost use of his legs ever to say, "I BELIEVE I can break the world long-jump record, therefore I CAN!" However, it would not be foolish for that same person to determine, "I BELIEVE I can become a famous author, and therefore I CAN!")

God works miracles. Humans do not. But God gives humans the ability to excel, and they can excel far above anyone else's expectation IF they believe they can. When people believe they are somebody special, they begin acting like somebody special, and eventually, with determination and drive, they can *become* somebody special.

A thirty-eight-year-old woman on welfare started reading a

book entitled *The Magic of Believing*. The more she read, the more she began to believe in herself. She recognized that she had a certain gift for making people laugh. She applied herself, and soon she was being paid for making people laugh, on a bigger and bigger scale. Her name is Phyllis Diller, and she eventually earned a million dollars a year just making people laugh. She always had a special talent, but when she finally recognized that talent, and started believing in herself, her life began to change.

Another example of achieving through self-belief is Roger Bannister. For over three thousand years, people around the world had run footraces, and no one had ever run a mile in less than 4 minutes. Breaking the 4-minute-mile barrier was thought to be impossible. But Bannister believed he could do it, and in May 1954, he recorded a 3:59:4 mile in England. Then other runners began to believe it was possible for them, too. Bannister's record was broken only forty-six days later by a miler named John Landy; and since then, more than five hundred men have raced a mile in less than 4 minutes! They did it because they *believed* they could!

Children are particularly susceptible to the influence of self-belief. Attitudes are habits, and children's attitudes of personal limitations are not as firmly set or deeply entrenched as those of adults. Children still have an ability to stretch their attitudes to include a wide variety of possibilities. A child still has a great imagination, which is a very important ingredient in self-belief.

My coauthor, Charles Paul Conn, illustrates this characteristic of children:

> Once, in Boston, I took my children to see an Ice Capades show in which the star skater was Olympic gold medalist Dorothy Hamill. The show was a bright and glamorous one, with swirl-

ing spotlights and spectacular costumes, and we were all cap-
tivated by the grace and beauty of the skaters.

A day or so later, sitting in our apartment, I looked up from
the newspaper I was reading to see six-year-old Heather gliding
across the living room floor. She was dressed in one of her
mother's pastel-colored slips, the straps wrapped carefully
around the head, as she shuffled across the carpeted floor with
a lurching stride. "What in the world are you doing?" I de-
manded in bewilderment. She paused to give me a puzzled
look, as if I had asked an exceptionally stupid question, and
answered without missing a beat, "I'm winning the gold medal
at the Winter Olympics!" And with that she skated, in her beat-
up sneakers, into the next room.

Children still have the ability to see themselves *as they might
become*, whereas most adults have become so convinced of the
impossible that their creative self-belief is impaired. The fortunate child is the one for whom a caring adult bolsters and
encourages that self-belief until it becomes a permanent habit
of thought called an attitude.

Here are some suggestions that you can use to help your
children learn to believe in themselves:

1. *Unconditional Love*

Give your children unconditional love. Always encourage
them and show that you love them even if they forget their
lines in the class play, drop the game-winning touchdown
pass, total the family car on the interstate, or choose to run
around with the wrong crowd. It is important for your children to know that you love them regardless of their mistakes,
shortcomings, or lapses of judgment.

2. *Believing in Your Children*

Tell them often that you believe in them. Express this by
sharing your expectations for them; giving them responsibil-

ities that contribute to the well-being of the family; helping them to acquire the knowledge and skills to be successful.

3. *Success Breeds Success*

Look for every possible way to provide opportunities for success in the home. Plan experiences appropriate to the age and interest level of your children. Encourage them always. Praise their successes—even their partial successes.

4. *Temporary Setbacks*

Help children learn to cope with temporary defeats or setbacks. Share with your children stories of successful people who have faced failures before becoming successful. Share with children how you as a parent overcame a setback. If children are going to learn to believe in themselves, they must learn that there are no failures, only temporary setbacks.

5. *Igniter Language*

Use expressions such as "You're special," "You can do it," and "I believe in you." These phrases ignite the spark of self-belief within each child. Avoid using "put-down" phrases that cause children to doubt themselves, phrases such as "You can't do anything right," "You'll never make it."

6. *Self-Acceptance*

Help your children to discover who they are and to like themselves so that they will be better prepared to handle the temporary setbacks in their lives. We can prepare them most effectively by communicating with them, guiding them, and continuously reassuring them, so that when they encounter serious difficulties they respond positively and do not lose faith in themselves.

7. *Accentuating the Positive*

Find out what your children's strengths are by observing them in different situations. Provide them with opportunities to participate in varied activities so they can discover their strengths and interests and the things that they like and do well. Encourage and support these interests. Reinforce their interests and strengths to build their self-confidence.

Somewhere along the way, most high achievers were inspired by adults who helped them believe they could be someone great. Flip Wilson, the comic, is a contemporary example. From his seat in the back of the classroom—where traditionally lazy, unmotivated students gravitate—Flip was moved to the front of the class. Why? he wanted to know. The classroom teacher told him it was because "I believe you can be a leader!" According to Wilson, those words from that teacher turned his life from "off" to "on." All he needed was to be told he could be someone great. When the teacher provided that spark, it was the catalyst he needed to move on to adult success.

One of my favorite stories is the one of a fellow named Bunker Bean. It is a story about a man who was tricked into believing in himself.

Unfortunately, many people pass through life selling themselves short. They spend their years putting all their time and energy into small tasks, never developing their innate potential to accomplish larger tasks.

Bunker Bean was once such a person. His parents died when he was a small child. He roamed the country in rags, passed from one foster family to another. He developed one of the world's most enormous inferiority complexes. His mind was full of fears. He was terrified of policemen. He hated elevators, disdained life, and was very pessimistic about his future.

Bunker lived in a cheap boardinghouse. There he met a spiritualistic medium who preached reincarnation. Bunker himself came to believe in reincarnation, and he idolized this new friend who seemed to have such insight into the secrets of life. Bunker agreed to pay the mystic if he could tell him who Bunker had been in a life prior to this one. After much fanfare and theatrics, the mystic revealed to Bunker that he had once been the great Napoleon Bonaparte, Emperor of France and conqueror of Europe.

Bunker wondered how he could be so timid and fearful in this life, having been such a powerful figure as Napoleon in a previous existence. The medium explained that life revolves in vast karmic cycles. As Napoleon he had lived in the ascendancy stage, which is characterized by courage and power. Now Bunker was living in the descendancy stage, which is characterized by fear and insecurity. However, the guru said that Bunker's cycle was about to reenter the ascendancy stage. He told Bunker that he would soon experience a strange stirring within himself, after which he would become an inspired, courageous, and forceful individual.

Just thinking of himself as Napoleon made Bunker feel like a million dollars. He stood upright and studied himself in the mirror. He felt a great wave of confidence surge within him. He began to read every book he could find about Napoleon, determined to recapture those positive qualities he had once possessed. He hung pictures of Napoleon on his walls. He imitated the dynamic leader's speech, thoughts, and actions. He meditated about important decisions. What, he asked himself, would I have done as Napoleon? He carefully planned his life, analyzing every problem and organizing his thoughts. He savored the knowledge that he possessed great personal power. There being no wars for this reborn Napoleon to fight, he decided he would apply his talents and positive attitude in the field of commerce. He focused on making money.

Bunker drove himself relentlessly. He believed, as Napoleon did, that "to think is to act!" Having acquired winning habits, Bunker enjoyed their rewards. People noticed a change in him; they began to pay attention to him. Bunker advanced rapidly in his work.

After a while, Bunker began to wonder who he had been prior to Napoleon. He returned to the mystic and offered him a great sum of money for the answer. Napoleon had lived only fifty-two years, after all, and it was important to Bunker to know about his previous existence.

For a fat fee, the mystic naturally had no difficulty in giving Bunker an answer. Prior to being Napoleon, he revealed, Bunker had been an Egyptian pharaoh, and he had lived a full life of eighty-two years as a man of great strength and leadership. He had been a mighty ruler, stern but just. He had also been tall and handsome, revealed the mystic.

Bunker was thrilled with this information. He immediately hired the best tailor he could find. He had his clothes cut to enhance his personal appearance and exerted effort to streamline his waist and develop his chest and shoulders. He sought to reacquire the regal appearance that had distinguished him in the pharaoh's body.

Acts of courage stiffened Bunker's spine. He felt important. He knew he was thinking boldly and could direct successful ventures. Never again, he told himself, would he allow fear and doubt to dominate his mind. Bunker Bean was a man aglow. As more and more positive thoughts entered his mind, it was like pouring phosphorus into his personality. But then . . .

One day Bunker Bean discovered that his friend the mystic was a total FAKE! Everything he had told Bunker was untrue. The shock was devastating, and Bunker wavered on the brink of collapse. But he did not buckle, because he had acquired winning habits, and habits are not easily broken. Bunker had learned the meaning of a great truth:

"As a man thinketh in his heart, so is he."

Bunker realized that when he had believed himself to be a nobody, he was. But when he believed himself to be a somebody, he *was* a somebody. Through changing his attitude about himself, he had become wealthy and successful; he had gained prestige and respect from others.

When Bunker Bean realized this truth, it didn't matter that the mystic had deceived him. It didn't matter whether life revolved in karmic cycles. He was his own person, a person of positive habits, a person who believed in his talents and skills. And now nothing could change that!

BELIEF-IN-SELF ACTIVITY

Unconditional love is total acceptance of ourselves and others.

Let's be ourselves! For example, select a day, once a week, on which each member of your family dresses exactly as he/she wants to dress. Accept Jimmy's choice to wear holey jeans and sneakers to dinner.

7 Self-confidence—Handmaiden of Success

A *handmaiden* is defined as that which accompanies in a useful but subordinate capacity. For example, it is often said that law is the handmaiden of justice—the instrument through which justice is achieved. Similarly, self-confidence is a means through which success is achieved; it is the handmaiden of success.

Several years ago, my wife and I entertained Dr. Norman Vincent Peale as a guest in our home. I was surprised, in conversation with him, to hear Dr. Peale confess that as a youth he was plagued with a severe sense of inferiority. He was shy and filled with self-doubt, constantly telling himself he was short on brains and ability. He was certain he would never amount to anything, and he lived in a miserable world

69

of self-deprecation. He realized that his classmates, his teachers, and virtually everyone he knew seemed to agree with his
low sense of self-worth. Even in college, he had difficulty
trying to socialize with persons outside the circle of his closest
friends.

One of Dr. Peale's ambitions had always been to be a public
speaker, but the thought of getting up in front of people
terrified him. He confessed to Carolyn and me that he still
experienced fear before a speaking engagement. However, he
would gain self-confidence by picking out a smiling face in
one of the front rows and focusing as much as possible on that
person. It was his way, he said, of convincing himself that
the person liked him and was interested in what he had to say.

A change occurred while Dr. Peale was still in college.
There, he had several professors who helped boost his self-
confidence. They reminded him constantly that he had great
potential and recommended that he read the works of Emer-
son and Marcus Aurelius, both of whom wrote on the control
and use of the human mind.

He remembers when he first began the conscious effort to
dismiss his defeatist feelings. The real breakthrough in
Dr. Peale's life as a self-confident individual came in 1933,
when he had completed his first year as pastor of Marble
Collegiate Church in New York City. He and his wife were
vacationing in England, and he spent the trip depressed and
burdened with worry that his rough first year as a pastor was
a harbinger of a bleak future in the ministry. Mrs. Peale
listened patiently as he dwelled on his discouragement, and
finally spoke back, firmly and emphatically: "Norman, you
are not only my husband but you're also my pastor, and I am
frankly disappointed in you. You talk from the pulpit about
faith, but I'm not seeing that quality in you now at all. In fact,

you're just whining about your defeat. What you need is to get your thinking straight. Believe in yourself. Think positively."

Dr. Peale found his wife's words so jolting and inspiring that he cut their vacation short and hurried back to his church duties in New York—eager and determined. He dove into his work with an awareness that he must express in his behavior a basic confidence in himself. He began to "act out" his positive ideas and apply them not just to others but *to himself as well!* The ensuing five decades speak to the remarkable difference that followed in his life.

When anyone lists the great proponents of positive thinking in America, a man named Zig Ziglar is always somewhere high on the list. But even with Zig, the battle for personal self-confidence was not won automatically. He was one of twelve children reared by his mother after his father died suddenly. He worked in a grocery store from the time he entered fifth grade until his senior year in high school, after which he did a short hitch in the army, then enrolled at the University of South Carolina. To work his way through college, Zig sold sandwiches in the dormitory at night and worked on a commission-only basis selling cookware. It was one of those "no sales, no pay" jobs, and he had a long series of ups and downs. There were times when he was penniless, discouraged, and frustrated.

Zig's life turned brighter when he met a man who convinced him that the only thing between him and great success was for him to believe in himself. He was hired by a man who expressed confidence in him and told him to start acting as if he were a winner rather than a loser. His self-confidence soared, and little more than a year later he became the number two salesman in a company of seven thousand salespersons! Zig says he was not necessarily working that much harder—

he had always worked hard—but was now working with a confidence that good things would result, and they did.

The late Napoleon Hill said: "One of the irreparable losses to the human race is the lack of knowledge that there is a definite method through which self-confidence can be developed in a person of average intelligence. . . . No one who lacks faith in himself is really educated in the proper sense of the word."

"Know thyself," the ancient philosopher advised us, and that knowledge includes being aware of one's own capacity for success and greatness.

Self-confidence is one side of a two-sided coin. The other side is fear: fear of failure, fear of embarrassment, fear that the good things life holds for other people will somehow elude us. The most debilitating thing about this kind of fear is that it prevents us from reaching out for the things we might be able to achieve. Fear of failure fosters an acceptance of failure; it keeps us from trying, and if we don't try, we don't succeed. So a vicious cycle is set up: fear produces failure; failure increases fear.

I once missed a great opportunity for precisely that reason: I was governed by fear rather than by optimism. My wife and I drove to Hilton Head Island to spend a weekend. Hilton Head is a beautiful resort area on the coast of South Carolina. During the drive, Carolyn and I commented at length on how our goals in life had changed. It had not been too far in the past that we had established a financial goal of earning $10,000 a year. Now we had reached the point at which we were driving to an island haven with an eye to buying a condominium there.

I had read countless books on positive thinking. They all encouraged thinking BIG. So Carolyn and I figured we should take our accountant's advice and THINK BIG—even though the prices of Hilton Head condos were mind-boggling to a couple who had spent their married life in the field of public education.

When we arrived at Hilton Head, we immediately called a realtor friend, who had promised to show us some bargain-priced property. He took us to one particular condo and said, "Billy, if it were not for the recent recession and its effect on the real estate market, this place we're looking at would sell for about $220,000–$225,000. As it is, you can buy it right now for only $125,000." All we had to do, he told us, was to put $25,000 down and mortgage the remaining $100,000. He was certain that in a year or so, when the market picked up again, we would be able to sell it for $75,000 to $100,000 more than we paid for it.

As a schoolteacher, the only time I dealt with figures like that was in math classes! I got excited! We decided to buy the condo, gratefully signed the contract and a check, and were on cloud nine the rest of the weekend. We felt fortunate to have a friend who would give us such a great deal.

Sunday evening, as we drove home, my wife said, "Billy, do you think we've done the right thing?" She raised the question of what we would do if something happened to my job, or if we were unable to rent the condo, or if the recession deepened. Once we began to think of things that might go wrong, the list of possible hazards seemed endless. The seeds of doubt had been planted, and I became horribly afraid I had made the wrong decision. It gnawed on me all the way home.

The first thing I did upon arriving home was to call the realtor at Hilton Head. I explained our apprehension. I told him I had always believed that if a person did not feel good inside about a decision, he shouldn't make it. So I asked my friend to tear up the contract and return our check. He told me he thought I was making a terrible mistake but would do whatever I asked.

A year later, we decided to go back to Hilton Head for another visit. We arrived to find that during the year, real estate sales had turned sharply upward. Our realtor friend told us he hated to say "I told you so," but he wanted us to see how the condo we had almost bought had turned out.

He showed us his ledger. The condo had sold only a short time before for a cool $220,000—$95,000 more than we had agreed to pay for it a year earlier. Looking at the figures made me almost physically sick with regret. Ninety-five thousand dollars—that was more money than I had made during the first ten years of my career in teaching and coaching. The news spoiled our weekend; as I recall, we left for home earlier than we had planned.

I told my wife, "Carolyn, let's make a pact never again to fill each other's heads with doubt and fear that will keep us from doing things we can do and want to do." By the following weekend, I had decided the best way to conquer fear was by taking action, so Carolyn and I drove to Myrtle Beach, which was closer to our home. There we found a condo we could afford, and this time we bought it! (That was ten years ago, incidentally, and we have never been sorry we made that purchase.)

Self-doubt is paralyzing. Self-confidence is mobilizing. Self-doubt prevents us from doing even those things that we do well; often it prevents us from doing anything at all, for fear that it will turn out badly. The only way to break out of a cycle of self-doubt is *action*. Do something! Select the action that has the highest likelihood of success, and do it! Then build on that success, until finally you are achieving the major victories of which you dream.

I was watching a crew of steelworkers erect a building one

day and particularly noticed two young men putting up steel
beams at least twenty stories above the ground. I knew the
beams were only twelve to eighteen inches wide, and it
amazed me how those workmen walked on the beams as if
they were on the ground. It seemed incredibly courageous.
Later, I walked over to a beam that was lying on the ground.
Very confidently I walked the length of it, never once losing
my balance on its foot-wide width. As I was doing so, however, I realized that if I had to walk it twenty stories up in the
air . . . well, I just couldn't do it, because I would be scared to
death.

That's when the thought struck me. The reason those workmen could do what I couldn't do was that they lacked fear. I
did not lack the dexterity to walk the beam—I had proved that
on the ground. The beam was the same width in the air as it
was on the ground. It was not nimble feet I lacked, but simple
self-confidence! Those steelworkers, believing in their own
ability, knew no fear, and each time they walked a beam, that
self-confidence grew. Each success adds to self-confidence,
which produces more success.

Self-confidence is cultivated in us by other people, especially in the beginning. The positive cycle of success breeding
self-confidence usually begins when someone else gives encouragement or expresses confidence. Obviously, no one is
more critical to that process in a growing child than the parent.
We do not encourage our children, and tell them of their
ability and potential, simply to give them an inflated opinion
of themselves, but so that they will dare to attempt things that
will in turn build their self-confidence.

How can parents build into their children a healthy self-
confidence? Here are a few practical suggestions:

1. Praise children for small acts of competence, beginning
at an early age.

2. Arrange "success experiences" for young children—tasks with a high likelihood of success—to give an expectation of positive results.

3. Avoid negative comparisons among siblings, even if you think that, in general, you balance out these comparisons. Remember that pointing out one child's shortcomings in comparison to a sibling's is not balanced by praising that child's positive qualities.

4. Let your children hear you praise others for behaviors that your children themselves demonstrate. In this way, your praise, generalized to the behavior of your own child, has greater credibility in being not a direct compliment but an indirect one. It is a way of letting your child "eavesdrop," in a sense. A warning: this indirect message works in both directions. If you call a ball player a dummy for striking out in a crucial situation, the child sitting beside you will assume that you also feel that way when he or she strikes out in a Little League game.

5. Pass on to your child compliments you hear from others. Do not fail to share the praise of others in fear that the child will become egotistical. If someone outside the family says good things to you about your children, let them enjoy it with you.

SELF-CONFIDENCE ACTIVITY

The positive cycle of success breeds self-confidence.

Weekly, allow your children to select specific activities that they want to master. For example, invite them to help you create a dessert for dinner. Allow them to make the selection, and reinforce their choice. Give them the opportunity to create it. Together, make the dessert. Along the way, offer praise.

8 Expectations—Anticipation of Success

People succeed or fail as a result of either their own expectations or the expectations of others.

Have you ever noticed how often bad news is accompanied by the expression, "That's just what I was afraid of!" When we fear bad things might happen, they usually do. When we predict failure, we usually fail. That is one of the most stable corollaries in all of human behavior. Conversely, when we expect success, we usually succeed.

One way of expressing this link between expectation and behavior is the phrase *self-fulfilling prophecy*. The individual predicts a certain outcome, then behaves in such a way as to fulfill his prediction, even when it is an outcome he greatly dislikes.

Another powerful phenomenon, called the *labeling effect*, expresses our tendency to behave in a way that corresponds to the labels attached to us by others. "If you persist in calling a child a thief," says one psychologist, "eventually he will begin to steal."

Psychologists have many other names for this well-established finding. In a research setting it is called the *Rosenthal effect*, named for the man who first described the phenomenon. If experimentalists expect subjects to behave in a certain way, they tend to behave that way, even when no other variable is at work.

The Rosenthal effect has been found to exist under an amazing variety of conditions. Educational psychologists have tested the effect by taking students identical in academic ability and dividing them randomly into two groups. If a schoolteacher is told that one set of students comprises "A" students and the other set "C" students, the teacher invariably begins to treat each group differently, and the students respond by performing differently. Soon the students' work becomes nearer and nearer the teacher's expectations; the "A" students do better work and the "C" students poorer work, based only on the subtle signals the teacher sends—that they are expected to perform in that way!

Expectation, however, is more than just a prediction; it is an attitude and, as such, is under our control. Expectation is simply the attitude of anticipating success or failure; it is a prophecy of what can and will happen. It is a mental and emotional *habit*. We must teach our children to anticipate great things in their lives, to get excited about those expectations, and to believe firmly that they will indeed come to pass.

Here are some guidelines that you can use to encourage your children toward high expectations.

1. *Evaluate Expectations*

Discuss yours and your children's expectations often to ensure that they are neither too high nor too low. Children want to live up to their parents' expectations, and they quickly incorporate those expectations. A six-year-old received a poor grade in reading. His parents, looking at the report card, told him that he *was not good* in reading. Since his parents believed he was not good in reading, he never *became* a good reader. Learn and evaluate your children's expectations, the labels they have begun to apply to themselves, to prevent the psychological damage of negative labeling.

2. *Monitor Your Behavior*

Be aware of the expectations that you have for your children. Be sure that the things you say and the actions you take communicate positive expectations only. Frequent checks on our conversations and actions help to prevent the unwitting but damaging expressions that may be interpreted as negative expectations. Finding fault with others will quickly teach children to do the same, and in turn to look for those same faults in themselves.

3. *Be Action Oriented*

Teach children to be action oriented, not to be afraid to take calculated risks, and not to be afraid of failure. Constantly encourage your children to try, even if they fall a little short. Children frequently avoid activities that they would really like to try (learning to play a musical instrument, trying out for a team or a role in a play) because of the fear of being criticized for not doing well or of not being selected. If they get knocked down, help them learn to *get up and try again!*

4. *Separate the Performance from the Performer*

There are going to be times when children do not live up to your expectations, and when you know that they can do better. Do not tear down the performer because of a poor performance. If you know your child can do better in his grades, or in the careless way he cuts the grass, let him know that you are not going to accept poor performance. Let him know that you have higher expectations for him. But be careful to let the child know that you are criticizing the performance and not the performer.

5. *Encourage a Feeling of Importance*

To help your children have high expectations, it is essential that you help them feel important and valued. Make an extra effort to help your children feel special and important by showing respect for them and by being kind and polite to them. Say nice things to them and treat them as the special people that they are. Seek their opinions and ideas about family matters. Always remember that *everybody* wants to be somebody special. If children are going to believe in themselves, it is essential that they feel important, and those feelings about themselves will be engendered first from the parents.

6. *Set the Example*

If a child is going to have high expectations, it is very important that parents have high expectations both for themselves and for their children. Expectation is the attitude of anticipation in life—the anticipation of good or bad, of success or failure, of positive or negative tomorrows. Cultivating positive or negative expectations is a habit. And habits are acquired through repetition. Repeated anticipation of the best from ourselves, the best from life, and the best from others forms one of life's most valuable habits.

7. *Expect the Best*

If you are going to expect children to have positive expectations in life, always expect the best of them. Do not become too impatient or too busy to transmit this expectation to your children. A by-product of today's busy, hectic lifestyle is the temptation for parents to compromise and accept less than the best because it is expedient.

Negative and positive expectations are powerful. A young girl, extremely talented in art, was labeled as average in school. She accepted that label and continued to function at that level because her parents never seemed to have the time to explore the reasons she was not performing up to what they thought were her real abilities. In contrast, there was the tall, lanky seventh-grade boy who had virtually no talent in basketball but was encouraged always to do his best. He translated his mother's and his coach's expectations into his own, and became a starter on the varsity basketball team; there had never before been a sophomore on the varsity squad.

When a person is guided by *positive expectations,* he begins to predict success as he taps the memories and conditioning of prior achievement. Guided by *negative expectations,* a person begins to prophesy failure as the recollections of previous failures undermine his self-confidence and he patterns his behavior to fail.

I know many golfers who have a particular bugaboo hole on the course they play regularly. The person arrives at the tee on his bugaboo hole and just KNOWS he'll hook his drive out of bounds, or slice it into a water hazard. Previous failures to hit the ball straight on this particular hole have accumulated to the point that he can't envision hitting his drive down the middle of the fairway.

Among the many differences between a pro golfer and the average weekend hacker is self-confidence. The pro steps up to the tee expecting to hit a good shot. He has hit so many that the few bad ones do not intrude.

In the 1984 Olympic Games in Los Angeles, gymnast Mary Lou Retton knew she was capable of executing a perfect vault and receiving a maximum score of ten. Although she couldn't be certain she would do so on that specific occasion, she did anticipate success because she had previously executed it successfully many times, both physically and visually. She was filled with self-confidence, and she EXPECTED to make it, and she did.

In the 1987 World Series, the Minnesota Twins entered the series with a lower winning percentage than any other team that had won the World Series in history. But they had been known all season as an unusually successful team when playing on their home field in the Metrodome. After five games of the series, they trailed the St. Louis Cardinals 3–2, but were scheduled to play the rest of the series in Minneapolis.

Twins players and coaches, though one game from defeat, entered the sixth game as if they couldn't lose; they were, after all, returning to the Metrodome, and they expected to win there. And win they did, sweeping all four of their home games.

Some sports commentators have speculated that the home-field "advantage," which operates in all sports, is due more to the home teams' positive expectations than to other tangible factors such as geography, crowd support, and familiarity with the environment.

Recently, I spoke with a newspaper reporter after making a speech in Pittsburgh. It was her observation that the performance of many reporters varied sharply with the types of assignments given them. When assigned to less significant stories, they tended to perform lackadaisically; when given major, demanding stories to cover, they responded with their best work. The reporter told me that being trusted with important assignments raised her own level of professional expectations, so she thought of herself as a big-time reporter and performed accordingly.

It has been known for many years that a physician's positive expectations are often communicated to a patient and become a factor in the speed of recovery. A common technique is the administering of a placebo, a medication having no significant effect on the disorder. The patient *thinks* he has been given a drug that will make him better, so he actually begins to get better, even though nothing at all has changed—except his expectation!

Charles Wilson, former president of General Motors, explained self-fulfilling prophecy as it applies in the world of business. The difference between a good boss and a poor boss, he said, is that a good boss makes workers feel they have more ability than they really do, thereby influencing them to do better work than they thought they could. In other words, he raises their expectations, and their actual performance follows suit.

The down side of this phenomenon is that a lack of high expectations from "significant others" can cause an individual to achieve far less than his potential. A classic example is that of Archie Griffin, an All-American football player who set a precedent by winning two Heisman trophies as a running back at Ohio State under the late coach Woody Hayes.

It was Ohio State whose team popularized the "three yards and a cloud of dust" approach to offensive football, which means that the emphasis was strongly on running the ball. The word *pass* never found its way into Coach Hayes's vocabulary. As a result, Archie Giffin was not very good at catching passes. He was drafted into the National Football League by the Cincinnati Bengals as a sturdy blocker and hard-nosed runner. He had never been EXPECTED to catch passes. When he reached the pros, Griffin had to work long and hard to become a back who could fake the run and be counted on to haul in passes as well. According to Griffin, becoming a leading NFL receiver was merely a matter of adjusting his expectations; as he experienced success as a receiver he began to believe he could excel at it, and it was not long before his quarterbacks EXPECTED him to be a pass-catching threat out of the backfield. He eventually became a premier receiver as well as a running back.

Another great pro football player victimized by the low expectations of others was Bob Lilly, a star tackle who became the first Dallas Cowboy to be voted into the Pro Football Hall of Fame. Lilly grew up as a big, strapping boy in football-crazy Texas. All that was ever expected of him was to be a rugged football player, a "dumb jock." Throughout high school and college, he was never expected to perform well academically; like other football players, he was assumed to be intellectually inept and was steered through soft courses that protected him from being challenged in the classroom.

Over the years, Lilly recalls, the stereotype of the dumb athlete was so often applied to him that he came to accept it as true. He wore the label so long that he believed it must fit. It was only after he left pro football and entered the business world that Lilly began to realize that he was, in fact, a very intelligent person. He retired from the Cowboys and went into a business that forced him to understand a complex merchandising system. In this new role he not only dealt with but met as an intellectual equal many whom he had perceived as his superiors. Today he is an extremely successful businessman, as shrewd and competent in the "head games" of that world as he was on the gridiron.

Over the years, I have frequently witnessed in my own life the importance of positive expectations. For the greater part of my early life, I programmed my mind to expect negative things. I was victimized by self-imposed limitations.

First, I came from a financially disadvantaged family. In elementary school, my negative expectations were so bad I didn't even want to go to school. I was afraid of taking tests, afraid of failing, afraid of being embarrassed. In the classroom I sought out the biggest kid so I could sit behind him and minimize my chances of being seen and called on by the teacher.

When I reached high school, things didn't improve much. I did have the expectation of receiving a diploma, but I had no ambitions as far as grades were concerned. I figured that C's and D's were good enough—just so I passed. Later, through the influence of significant others, I became determined to go to college and began to aspire toward reasonably good grades. As my expectations rose, I began making better grades; soon, making passing grades was no longer satisfactory to me. My expectation was to make A's and B's, and this expectation, too, became a reality.

The change that occurred as a result of this newly found positive attitude was shocking to those who had known me and taught me in school. Eventually, I entered Birmingham Southern, a highly rated liberal arts college, and completed four years of study in only two years and seven months. After that I moved on to a master's degree and a doctoral degree in education. Each time I elevated my expectations and achieved them, I reinforced my self-confidence and in turn established even higher levels of expectation.

It is a chain reaction, an upward spiral in which expectation of success and the success itself nurture each other.

In 1980 I talked with Bruce Jenner about his gold medal performance in the decathlon in the Olympics earlier that year. Four years before, he had been defeated in the same event. He attributed that defeat in large measure to his expectation *not* to win. He told me his mind had been programmed for failure in 1976. Realizing that, he set out to prepare for his rematch with the world's greatest athletes by focusing on the message, "I CAN win, I WILL win!"

He set numerous specific subgoals, calculated the levels of performance necessary to win the grueling ten-event competition, and entered the 1980 Olympics ready to run and jump with total confidence that, this time, he would win the gold medal. He had the expectation of winning, and he won, setting a new world record in the process.

Keep in mind that expectation is not simply wishful thinking. One doesn't say to oneself, "I've been a loser *x* number of times, so it's my turn to win." Instead, one works to make victory possible. Then, believing that victory will follow, one experiences less conflict, strife, turmoil, despair, and anxiety as the moment of truth approaches.

Dr. Norman Vincent Peale has said that the power of self-fulfilling prophecy can work two ways, either *for* you or *against* you—but it always works.

EXPECTATIONS ACTIVITY

*Always expect the best from yourself as well as
from your children!*

Play a game together. Do your best. If you have had fun, you have won!

---

9 Goals—Targets of Success

What comes first, the chicken or the egg?

Does a child first expect to succeed, and then do so? Or does he first succeed, and then expect to do so again? Obviously, the process is mutually self-starting, which means that nothing is more beneficial to the young child than to experience some sort of success as early and as often as possible.

To build into your child's attitude a pattern of positive expectation, it is necessary that he be given a way of "keeping score." Children know they are doing well when the task itself is well defined and the goals are clearly stated. *Goals are the targets of success.* How can the child experience the thrill of hitting the bull's eye when he doesn't know what the target is? Or, in the words of the outstanding management expert

89

Bill Britt, "If you don't know where you're going, how will you know when you get there?"

Children need to be taught to translate an expectation of success into specific, tangible goals that allow them to see for themselves their hits and their misses. Goal setting is the way we teach kids to convert a positive general attitude into concrete accomplishment.

Can you imagine a hockey game being played without a net on each end of the rink? Just as nets give purpose to the game of hockey, goals give purpose to our lives. Children must learn to set goals—immediate, short-range, and long-range goals, realistic and attainable—and then use those goals as the scorecard that they trust, rather than the opinions of others or some vague sense of how they are doing.

I cannot overemphasize the need to distinguish between a general expectation of success (dreaming, in the best sense), and the setting of specific goals. The ability to dream, to envision great things, to expect success, is critical to any form of significant achievement. But expecting great things to happen in one's life makes sense only when one sets specific goals to bridge the gap between the dream and the reality.

Unfortunately, our society frequently punishes the child who dreams big dreams and dares to express them. To admit to positive expectations is often regarded as boastful or arrogant. We are expected to drape our hopes for the future with a certain veil of false humility as we expose them to public view.

Charles Paul Conn, writing about this pressure *not* to aspire, says:

> Somehow, by some perverse logic, there is a sentiment that argues that all men are created equal and should always remain

equal in every way, that somehow for an individual to seek to be better than the crowd is undemocratic, un-Christian, unseemly, and just downright neurotic! We have all felt the subtle pressure to apologize for our successes in the classroom or on the job or in the community or even in our own families. It is important not to succumb to that pressure. People who work hard to reach personal goals are better persons than they were before . . . and there is nothing wrong with striving toward that.

One of the wonderful things about children is that they are so open about the things they want. No one has taught them yet to be restrained and cautious in expressing their expectations. Boldly, enthusiastically, they describe the wonderful, glittering future that lies before them. "When I grow up, I'm gonna be an astronaut!" (Doesn't he realize the odds are a million to one against it?) "When I grow up, I'm gonna be a movie star!" (Hasn't anyone told her how unlikely that is?) "When I grow up, I'm gonna be president of the United States!" (Sure, kid, now eat your oatmeal.)

Chris Andersen, senior editor of *People* magazine, recalls this incident:

> I was never shy about being ambitious. When my ninth-grade social studies teacher asked us on the first day of class to scribble down what we wanted to achieve in life, I did not hesitate. He read through a number of answers aloud, then began glossing over them when it became clear that nearly all the responses sounded like speeches delivered by semifinalists in the Miss Universe Pageant. ("I want to bring peace and understanding to people of the world. . . .") Then he came to mine: "Wealth, fame and power—though not necessarily in that order." He thanked me for supplying the day's only honest answer.

Kids have not yet learned to fear ridicule if the expectations to which they admit are too high. Instead of discouraging their dreams, parents should teach them how to set specific intermediate goals that will move them along the path from where they are to where they want to be.

These are some techniques that you can use to help your children learn to set and attain their goals:

1. *Dreams and Goals*

Encourage your children to dream. Help them to jot down their dreams and goals. Assist them, if needed, in writing their goals on an index card. Post the index card in their bedroom or another appropriate location where they will see and review the goals daily.

2. *Priorities*

Help your children to prioritize their goals. Have them consider their goals in the order of their importance. Place beside each written goal a proposed target date for attainment of that goal.

3. *Planning*

Help children think about how they can make their goals become reality. Help them think about the obstacles or difficulties they must overcome to attain their goals, or how they may avoid them. Help them prepare a "people plan" within their plan—which people are needed to help them attain their goals, and what they will do. Prepare a timetable for reaching the goals. For example, if a child wants to become a doctor, discuss how long this will take, what one must do to become a doctor, courses that must be taken, and other requirements that must be met.

4. Daily "Do List"

Show children how to prepare a daily "do list." In the evening, prepare a list of six to ten things children would like to do the following day. Date the card and allow space on the right side of the card where they can check off what they have accomplished. At the end of each day, help them to review the progress they have made that day. Have an index file-box to file the daily cards. At the end of one month, six months, and at the end of the year, the children can review all that they have accomplished during that time period, strongly reinforcing the idea that they can set and achieve goals.

5. Visualization

Help children to learn to concentrate, to learn to use the powerful motivating force of visualization. Find a quiet time— morning, noon, or evening—to visualize their goals and dreams. Encourage the daily use of visualization so that it may become a habit. Help children to see in their imagination the things they want to accomplish, where they want to be, and the ideas they want to have.

6. Teamwork

Help children to understand that achieving goals is frequently a team effort. Sometimes we need the special skills and insights of others if we are going to achieve our goals. For example: a child who wants to be a member of a team may need parents or older brothers or sisters to drive him to the pool or the ball park. All family members may have to sacrifice some of the things they want while paying for one or more of the family to go to college. When goals are reached, be sure there is a celebration of the accomplishment. Give special recognition to the one whose goal was achieved, but assure a sense of involvement and satisfaction for the whole family.

Abraham Maslow, the great psychologist who studied the nature of creativity, wrote that the common quality found in most highly creative individuals is a certain type of *childlikeness* that allows them to explore and manipulate novel ideas and combinations of ideas that other, more "mature" persons overlook.

That is the childlike characteristic that parents should seek to preserve, while balancing it with an intelligent awareness of whether goals are realistic and attainable.

You cannot expect to hit an archery target with a bow and arrow from two blocks away—it is beyond the physical capabilities of the equipment. We must know the limits of our human equipment if we are to establish and attain personal goals. It is true, of course, that a goal that seems unattainable today may become a realistic goal tomorrow, depending on how well we cultivate our talents to attain it. One who has been physically inactive cannot expect to complete a marathon run. But he can condition himself to jog a block, then a quarter mile, then two miles, and eventually the marathon goal is a reasonable expectation.

Parents who discourage the excessive expectations of their children do so for very good reason, of course: they don't wish their children to set such high goals that they are setting themselves up for disappointment, or are putting such pressure on themselves that they might crumble under it. Here, as in so much of parenting, balance is the key. A parent must encourage the child to dream big dreams and expect excellence, all the while making sure that the pressure to excel comes from the child himself.

We have all heard horror stories about overzealous parents who *overexpect* and who teach their children to do the same, so that the least amount of failure is devastating. Psychiatrist Paul Meier tells of such a case:

> I have seen this emphasis get out of hand in some of the families I have dealt with. I had a patient with a Ph.D. from Duke University who frequently felt like a failure because he didn't go after an M.D. degree, as his parents had wished. I know another man with a doctorate in economics from Harvard, who is very successful professionally and a brilliant scholar. But he still carries around bad feelings about the one course in which he didn't get an "A" as an undergraduate in college. His parents had taught him that anything less than an "A" is a dishonor to the entire family. His uncle even flew in from out of state to talk to him about it when it happened. If we as parents have unrealistic expectations for our children, they will feel like failures, no matter how much they succeed in the world's eyes.

How can we decide whether dreams—either our children's or our own—are realistic? Try this gauge: a dream is attainable only if a set of specific goals can be set which, when completed, will result in the dream's being realized.

The story is told of a motorist who stopped along the side of the road to ask a farmer for directions to a neighboring town. Sure, the farmer said, he had heard of the town; it was in the next county, about twenty miles away.

"Can you tell me the best way to get there?" the motorist asked.

The farmer did not respond for several moments, chewing thoughtfully on a straw, as he pondered the question. Finally, with a puzzled look and a shrug of frustration, he replied, "Well son, as I think about it, I reckon you just ain't gonna be able to get there from here!"

That is the way it is with some ambitions. Sometimes you "ain't gonna get there from here." Goals are the vehicles that get us there, and learning to set them is a necessary part of the training of a high-achieving child. Goals are important to us because they:

- help us identify what is realistic
- focus our attention on effort
- serve as yardsticks in measuring progress
- help us become more efficient as we proceed

Successful goal seeking is simply a matter of forming building blocks into an ultimate pyramid. The question naturally arises: if setting goals and attaining them is so easy, why is the world full of so many failures?

The answer is that only 3 percent of all people formulate goals and action plans, and actually put them in writing. Ten percent have unwritten goals and plans. The rest of the population drifts through life with no explicit goals or action plans whatever!

A great motivator, Glen Bland, states that the 3 percent of people who have written goals and plans accomplish from fifty to one hundred times more during their lives than the 10 percent who have goals but do not commit them to writing. He says, "Men who have goals and plans dictate to others, while men who have no goals or plans are dictated to."

This does not mean you can sit down tonight, set some goals for yourself, jot down a plan of action, and tomorrow take over your boss's job! The missing ingredients are hard work, dedication, and insulation against self-doubt and occasional roadblocks. But by setting goals and making plans—and committing them to writing—you can expect to become a better decision maker, develop greater self-confidence, create and sustain a higher level of self-motivation, suffer less confusion about where you're going and how you'll get there, and enjoy bit-by-bit doses of success from day to day.

GOALS ACTIVITY

Over 90 percent of people who write
down their goals achieve them!
You can, too!

Every Sunday, write a goal for the week. Post it. Encourage one another through daily reinforcement. For instance, my goal is "I do not want to eat after 8:00 P.M." Each day someone in my family helps me achieve my goal by positive reinforcement such as, "Let's go for a walk instead of having our evening snack." By using this supportive communication daily, I know that I will achieve my goal!

10 Self-esteem—Feelings of Success

Self-esteem comes from within, as the word itself implies. It is the sum total of all of a person's feelings about himself—not the information he has about himself but his involuntary, conscious, and unconscious feelings.

One's self-esteem, though it is internally generated, has many of its origins in the opinions of others. Self-esteem is drawn primarily from a perception of what others think. There is an old saying: "I am not what I think I am; I am not what you think I am; I am what I think you think I am." That is not just a tongue twister; it expresses the fact that my feelings about myself are largely a reflection of what I think *your* feelings about me are.

Our attitudes toward and about our children have an amazing power to surface in the form of their own self-esteem. Our view of them becomes their own perception of themselves, whether that view is accurate or inaccurate.

Richard DeVos, in his book *Believe!*, shares an anecdote that illustrates the point:

> One time I drove my car into a service station to get some gasoline. It was a beautiful day and I was feeling fine. As I walked into the station, a young chap standing there said, rather unexpectedly, "How do you feel?"
>
> I said, "I feel wonderful."
>
> "You look sick," he said. Get the picture: this fellow wasn't a medical doctor; he wasn't an internist; he wasn't a male nurse.
>
> I answered him, maybe a little less confidently this time, "No, I feel fine. I never felt better."
>
> He said, "Well, you don't look so good. Your color is bad. You look yellow."
>
> Well, I left that gas station, and before I had driven a block, I stopped the car and looked in the mirror to see how I felt! After I got home I kept checking for pale color, yellow jaundice, something, anything! I thought, maybe I don't feel all right after all. Maybe I have a bad liver. Maybe I'm sick and I just don't know it.
>
> The next time I went to that gas station I figured out what the problem was: they had just painted the station a sick-looking yellow, and everybody who went into the place developed a ghastly yellow look!
>
> The point is that I had let one comment from one total stranger change my whole attitude for the rest of the day. He told me I looked sick, and before I knew it I was actually *feeling* sick!

The feeling is the thing. Self-esteem is not what one *thinks* about oneself so much as how one *feels* about oneself, and that is often a reflection of what one perceives to be the opinions of others.

The Sumter District Two school experience was based on the feelings children had about themselves, more than on any other single factor. The major problem was that they felt they were losers, and we set out to change that. The key was the "significant other" adults; when we taught those adults how to act as though they saw the kids as winners, the kids began to feel like winners and hence behaved accordingly.

If I have a single goal for this book, it is to help parents begin to do in their own homes their own smaller version of the POPS systematic program I described in chapter 2. Most parents take very seriously their need to provide the material necessities for their children. Very few of us—certainly no one reading this type of book—would fail to provide food, clothing, and a warm place to sleep at night.

Although my interest in self-esteem training was triggered by my role as an educator, I have since come to understand that *parents* are the true teachers of life. What they teach their children about self-worth is far more important than any lesson taught in school.

It is necessary that a parent provide for a child the raw material from which self-esteem is developed. Author Gordon MacDonald, in *The Effective Father*, explains parental responsibility this way:

> Family life is an existential classroom; it lasts for about eighteen years. Within the classroom are children who are like large lumps of clay. The longer they live, the harder the clay will become unless the potter consciously sustains the molding process, keeping the clay pliable—"shapeable."
>
> Each day the effective father stamps into the lives of his children words, attitudes, habits, and responses which one day

will become automatic. It would be frightening if a father did not realize this fact. For teach he will—whether he is aware of it or not. Ironically, teaching can be done either through design or negligence. Teaching, conscious or unconscious, will make an indelible impression upon a child's personality and become part of a composite of future character performance. The weaknesses and flaws of the father will be passed on to the children in either case. So the question confronts us: Do we teach to build or teach to cripple?

The tendency of the child with low self-esteem is always to withdraw from the setting in which failure might occur. Somehow we must draw that child into situations in which success is likely, so that a taste of success will gradually start the cycle.

Here are eight strategies for building your child's self-esteem:

1. Give positive support to your child by smiling at him when he talks or giving him a "pat on the back" whenever it is appropriate.

2. Demonstrate acceptance by using such phrases as "I like the way you . . ." or "It looked as if you enjoyed . . ." or "I know you must feel good when you. . . ."

3. Send your child a greeting card just to show your affection.

4. Give your child a hug, a kiss, or a loving touch when he is not expecting it.

5. Let your child be a child; don't rush his development.

6. Support your child's hobbies and interests by giving him praise and encouragement.

7. Ask your child to teach you a skill he has learned.

8. Assign your child chores that challenge him and that are within his capabilities but are beyond his usual range of activity.

There was a young girl in my school system who was so shy she simply froze at the thought of getting up and talking before a group. She asked to be excused from giving oral reports in class. Her teacher honored her request, but she asked the girl to begin practicing at home, in front of a mirror and in front of her parents. The teacher asked that the girl then meet with her after school several times a semester and practice speaking to her as though she were the entire class. The teacher kept encouraging this shy, reluctant youngster and offering praise as she improved. It took a year, but finally the student had developed sufficient self-confidence to speak quite eloquently before her classmates.

I have a friend whose daughter Heather gained that treasured teenage commodity, a driver's license, at age sixteen, but did not know how to drive a car with manual transmission. She had tried to learn how to shift gears, but was not learning rapidly and had become intimidated by the whole process. She decided to deal with the problem simply by vowing not to drive the snappy little sports car the family owned—and which she loved—and instead to confine her driving to the family sedan with automatic transmission.

At this point the mother stepped in and laid down a firm rule: you drive the stick shift or nothing. Not having a way to avoid the pain of learning this new thing, Heather set out once again to learn gear shifting, and literally by the end of the day was dashing happily around town in the red sports car, doing something she had just pronounced herself unable to learn!

The payoff for Heather was a double one, of course. Not only did she gain the specific skill of being able to drive a stick-shift car; but, far more important, she learned *the experience of success!* She learned that a difficult task, if tackled without reservations, can be mastered. That is the stuff of which self-esteem is made. The trick, for the parent, is to know when a task is truly within the child's reach and to participate in the learning process with the child, giving the necessary support until the child is able to function alone.

The payoff for the parent is that such success experiences give an opportunity to smother the child with honest praise and recognition for a job well done, and that keeps the development of self-esteem going.

Admiration and recognition from those close to us is a key in the process. In general, children see themselves as others see them. They treat themselves as others treat them. They value themselves as others value them.

The parent tells the child how much he is worth by expressing the value that he or she, the parent, personally places on the child. That is how self-esteem is learned. When we show the child we place little value on him, we are bequeathing to him a low self-esteem. That is what MacDonald means when he uses the phrase "teach to cripple." There are millions of children and adolescents who, like Charlie Brown, look into the mirror of life and see reflected back at them someone just not right for the part.

In my many years of working with young people, I have seen nothing more devastating than a feeling of low self-esteem. Every time I hear a parent berating his child in public—or an adult demeaning his spouse—I want to take that individual aside and relate this charming story. It is a story about how to build, rather than tear down, self-esteem.

Johnny Lingo lived in a primitive culture. It was one in which a young man desiring a particular maiden for his bride bargained with her father, who traditionally expected payment for his daughter. Payment was usually in cows. Two or three cows for an above-average wife was the going rate; an exceptionally beautiful wife sometimes brought four or five cows.

Johnny Lingo was the brightest, strongest, most handsome young man in the village. But it happened that the apple of his eye was a plain-looking girl—not ugly, but plain at best. Her name was Sarita, and she was shy, frightened of her own voice, and afraid to speak or laugh in public. Yet Johnny Lingo loved Sarita; so he went to her father and bargained for her hand in marriage.

As he did, the villagers speculated how many cows Sarita would bring for the father. Most figured it would be two, possibly three, and they laughed that Sarita's father would probably have little choice but to settle for even one cow. Imagine their shock when Johnny went before Sarita's father and told him, "Sir, I offer eight cows for your daughter."

Eight cows! It was the highest price ever paid for a bride in that village. But Johnny Lingo stood by his word, and the wedding took place. As the story goes, Sarita underwent a startling transformation. Within a few months, she developed the bearing of a queen, moving with striking grace and poise. The sparkle in her eyes was dazzling. People who visited the village and had not known Sarita before called her the most beautiful woman in the entire kingdom.

Much later, Johnny Lingo was asked why he had paid such an unheard-of price for Sarita. Someone with his masculine attributes and his shrewdness as a trader could certainly have obtained Sarita for much less.

Johnny explained that, yes, he did it partially to make Sarita happy. "But I wanted more than that. Many things can change a woman, things that happen inside as well as outside. And what matters most is what a woman thinks about herself." Johnny reminded the listener that before the marriage Sarita believed she was worth nothing. But knowing she was worth more than any other woman in the village, she looked and acted accordingly. Johnny Lingo concluded: "I loved Sarita. I wanted to marry her more than anything else in the world. But, I also felt I deserved an eight-cow wife!"

There is a simple formula for the development of a productive lifestyle: positive *thoughts* produce positive *feelings;* positive feelings make possible positive *behaviors,* which produce positive *consequences.* To start this cycle in our children's lives, it is critical that we help them experience success, however small, and however hard we must work to concoct the conditions under which that success experience will occur.

SELF-ESTEEM ACTIVITY

Daily self-love.
If I love myself, I can do anything!

At dinner have family members join hands and simply state something they felt good about during the day. Talk about why that feels good inside. The beauty of this activity is that you can do it at any time and any place.

11 Communication—Essential for Success

Dale Carnegie said that the primary rule for good communication is to talk less and listen more. If that is true between two adults, it is even more true between parent and child. Good parent-child communication begins as parents learn to hear what children are saying and to encourage them to say more.

An Atlanta sportswriter once wrote of Pepper Rodgers, the Georgia Tech football coach, "Pepper has a speech impediment; he doesn't know how to listen."

Many parents have that same kind of "speech impediment"; they spend so much of their time talking *at* their children and *to* their children and *about* their children that they rarely take time to hear *from* their children.

As a coach, I was sometimes regarded by parents as something of a Pied Piper for the young men with whom I worked. High school athletes had a tendency to become attached to me in a strong and personal way. This certainly made me a more effective coach, and it also increased my ability to influence the students in nonathletic ways as well. Students were drawn to me not necessarily because I was a better-than-average coach but more likely because I always took time to listen to them, to hear them out, to find out what they were saying and thinking.

Psychologist Robert Fisher, in *The Language of Love*, tells an amusing story that shows the degree to which listening is a major part of the whole process of communication. As a college student, he was hitchhiking in California and was picked up by a solitary motorist.

> As we began to journey together, he started talking and I started listening. To my surprise, as I paid close attention to what he was saying, I found myself genuinely interested and involved in the conversation. Occasionally I would make a comment or ask a pertinent question, but I was never asked and never gave any information about myself. The time passed quickly and soon we were in Bakersfield. We came to the crossroads where he was to turn off. Instead, he decided to take me to another main intersection ten miles or so further on where he thought my chances of getting a ride would be better. As we traveled on, he kept talking and I kept listening. When we arrived at our new destination, he remarked that he had never seen so few cars on the road. I might have a difficult time getting picked up there, he said, so he would take me to the base of the Ridge Route . . . that was another fifteen miles. He kept talking; I kept listening.
>
> As we came to the Ridge Route he had to make a decision. Was he going to take me over the mountain into Southern

California (about 75 miles) or was he going to let me out, turn around, and go back home? "I can't believe this traffic," he said. "You know, I don't have anything important to do today. I'm going to take you on over the mountain." An hour or so later we arrived in the San Fernando Valley.

During all our time together he had never asked me anything about myself, not even my name. He had told me about his family, his business, his dreams and ambitions. I forgot about trying to impress him by telling him about myself. I found it interesting and stimulating to learn so much about another person. I thoroughly enjoyed the conversation. . . . As I got out and was about to close the car door, he stopped me.

"Just a minute, young man. Before you go I want to tell you something. I make a habit of picking up hitchhikers. I like to learn about other people. I enjoy a good conversation." He paused and became more serious. "I know you're young," he said, "but I want you to know you are absolutely one of the finest conversationalists I have ever met."

Many of our children would think we had suddenly become great conversationalists if we just stopped talking and began *listening* to them for a change. We might be surprised at some of the things we would learn. For those times of conversation with our children, here are a few guidelines for effective communication, according to Dr. James Mallory, a psychiatrist who specialized in family therapy:

1. *Avoid "collective monologue."*

This is the kind of conversation in which the two parties are not really exchanging ideas at all, but merely engaged in two separate monologues. One makes a short speech, then waits for the other to make a short speech before it is his turn again. This is not dialogue at all, and very little real communication occurs. Good conversation is like a tennis match; when the person with whom you are playing hits the ball to you, you hit

it back to him. In collective monologue, this doesn't happen;
instead, both players are throwing balls up into the air and
hitting them past the other person.

2. *Seek to address the problem rather than ascribing blame.*

In most cases, whom to blame for a problem is a nonconstructive question to begin with. Blame placing wastes time
and creates negative feelings all the way around. It is far better
to move immediately to the problem at hand: what do we do
from here?

3. *Don't come on immediately with advice.*

The parent who responds to his child's dilemma with pat
answers is sending the message to his child that he doesn't
regard the problem as being very difficult or complex. It
implies that the problem is too simple. Even if you think you
know the solution to the child's problem it is a good idea to
wait awhile, listen while the child fully explores all aspects of
the situation, then give advice if it is appropriate to do so.
Often the child will talk his way through to the same solution
you would have given, and in this case will be far more ready
to accept it.

4. *Be confidential.*

This is a good practice not only for professional counselors
but for parents as well. Many well-intentioned parents discourage their children from confiding in them by spreading the
information to friends, neighbors, or other family members.
One of the greatest inhibitors of good communication, especially with young people, is fear of being exposed and embarrassed. Children learn quickly whether their parents can
be trusted to hold information in confidence, and having that
trust can be valuable to family communication at every level.

5. *Please touch.*

Body language is important in all kinds of communication,
and between parent and child it is particularly so. A touch, a

pat on the shoulder, an embrace—all can be effective ways of breaking down the barriers of communication that sometimes develop between parents and their growing children. This is obviously easier with a teenager if one has been physically affectionate throughout the child's life, but it is never too late to begin showing physical closeness when communicating with children. Touching signals closeness and intimacy, and many children need such expressions like thirsty plants need water.

6. *Don't feel you must point out all the inconsistencies in a child's statements.*

Children and teenagers are not fully developed yet in a cognitive and intellectual sense, and there are commonly gaping holes in their logic, particularly when they are emotionally involved in something they are trying to communicate. Too many parents feel called upon to point out every inconsistency in the child's story. If these lapses of logic are critical to the decision that is being made or to the point under dispute, it may be necessary to address them. But if they are simply adolescent overstatements, or if they issue from the whimsical and changing opinions of a child, it serves no good purpose to point them out. All that does is make the parent a sort of "logic cop," which may satisfy the parent's sense of order but does not encourage open communication from the child.

7. *Don't finish your child's sentences.*

In any conversation, it is offensive to interrupt the speaker to finish his or her sentence. Some adults are particularly prone to this when talking to children or teenagers. Because children are so unpredictable, you will frequently miss the point by barging ahead. Moreover, children are more easily intimidated into silence, and are more likely to quit talking altogether, if they are constantly preempted by an adult who rushes them along by anticipating what they will say next. It is important to give the child verbal feedback to let him know you are listening, but that feedback should not "lead" him.

8. *Don't play the role of district attorney.*

This means that the parent should stifle the urge to dig for details beyond those volunteered by the child. Communication between parents and their children often becomes a verbal tug-of-war, with the parents trying to pull from the children more information than they wish to disclose. If this occurs frequently, the child will stop opening up at all. If a child tells you A, and you insist on knowing B and C, the child will soon learn not to bring up the subject to begin with. Here is the most familiar of all parent-child exchanges: "Where did you go?" "Out." "What did you do?" "Nothing." Does that bit of dialogue sound familiar? It is the common case of the parent digging for details the child doesn't want to give. It is better to take an interest, responding in an interested but nonprosecutorial fashion, and you may be amazed at how much information is ultimately volunteered.

9. *Encourage your child to expand on what he says.*

This is different from digging for more details, for here the adult is not seeking information beyond what is offered but rather asking questions that encourage the child to elaborate on his feelings and opinions about things he has already said. "Why do you feel that way?" "It sounds as if you feel strongly about this." These are the types of responses that elicit additional expression without seeming to push for more disclosure.

10. *Don't resort to euphemisms.*

In communication with children, it is especially important to say what you mean rather than to cloak every utterance in allusion and innuendo. A child is not as adept at subtlety and reading between the lines as adults are, and it is possible for parents to leave a conversation feeling that they have said one thing while the child has heard something entirely different. Talking with your children is no time for veiled references and vague ideas. Be explicit; make sure the child understands the words and concepts you are using. Don't assume that he automatically understands the metaphors and socially accepted code words that other adults find familiar.

Research shows that the average parent spends less than sixty seconds a day with each child in a one-to-one conversation. The most serious problem in communicating with our children, therefore, is not that we do it poorly but that we simply do not do enough of it.

At the heart of good family relationships is healthy communication. Parents who can communicate effectively with their children are generally parents who can solve family problems as they arise, and whose values are most likely to be transmitted to the next generation.

COMMUNICATION ACTIVITY

Reading and writing are exciting!
Make it a habit!

Take turns reading to one another. Ask each other questions about what you have read. Also, write about what you have read to reinforce communication.

12 Human Relations—Necessary for Success

One of the areas in which I was least skillful as a father was in teaching my two young boys the value of good human relations. In fact, I probably did them more harm than good because I actually taught them to fight!

When I was growing up in the steel-mill town of my childhood, fighting was the natural way of interacting for school-boys. If you didn't get along with someone, or if you had an argument about something, you dropped your books and fought. That's just the way it was. It was the way a boy earned respect.

When my own two sons reached school age, I felt it was important to teach them not to let anyone take advantage of them, so I taught them to fight. I taught them how to box and wrestle—not to be on the wrestling or boxing team but simply to hold their own with other boys! Fortunately my wife had a better understanding of human relations than I did and helped teach them more appropriate ways to deal with their peers.

While we give so much attention to teaching children self-esteem, self-confidence, and positive attitudes about themselves, it is important that we also teach them how to deal with other people. The most self-assured youngster in the world can be a total failure if he has not learned how to interact positively with others.

Parents can help their children build and improve good human relations skills.

1. Teach your children early in life to use basic good manners in any kind of social situation.

2. Encourage your children to be good listeners—to make eye contact and to use body language to show that they understand what's being said.

3. Practice the Golden Rule, and teach children to do the same.

4. Provide appropriate opportunities for your children to learn to feel comfortable in small and large groups.

5. Teach your children to ask others, "What do you think?"

6. Stress the importance of tact.

7. Help your children learn to praise others and recognize their accomplishments.

8. Value good, positive social relationships, and encourage your children to do so.

9. Encourage your children to be unselfish. They must learn to give, to share, and to be considerate of others.

10. Provide the home environment that will enable your child to admit, "I made a mistake."

11. Stress to your children the importance of not "telling tales."

Children learn how to treat others based primarily on the way they are treated by their own parents. It has long been understood by experts in child abuse that a very high percentage of child abusers were abused themselves as children. Even though a child is scarred by the effects of an abusive parent and may harbor great anger at the treatment suffered at the hands of that parent, there is still a high likelihood that he or she will become, as an adult, an abusive parent.

Children are extremely sensitive to the offenses committed against them by their parents, sometimes even unfairly so. It is not difficult to bruise a child's feelings and hardly even know it, and in doing so to teach the child a permanent lesson about how to treat others in an offensive manner.

Gary Smalley is a writer who is particularly insightful on the topic of how parents model offensive behavior in their interaction with their children. In *The Key to Your Child's Heart* he says:

> As you seek to discover how you might have offended your child, you may need some help coming up with some possibilities. In my counseling and work with children around the country, I have asked many of them how their parents have offended them. Here are their actual responses:
>
> 1. Lacking interest in things that matter to me.
> 2. Breaking promises.
> 3. Criticizing unjustly.
> 4. Allowing my brother or sister to put me down.
> 5. Misunderstanding my motives.
> 6. Speaking carelessly.

7. Punishing me for something for which I had already been punished.
8. Telling me that my opinions don't really matter.
9. Giving me the feeling that they never make mistakes.
10. Not being gentle when pointing out my weaknesses or blind spots.
11. Lecturing me and not understanding, when all I need is some support.
12. Never telling me "I love you." Never showing me physical affection.
13. Not spending time alone with me.
14. Being insensitive, rough, and breaking promises.
15. Being thoughtless.
16. Never telling me "thank you."
17. Not spending time together.
18. Being insensitive to my trials.
19. Speaking harsh words.
20. Being inconsistent.
21. Taking me for granted.
22. Telling me how to do something that I was doing on my own.
23. Nagging me.
24. Bossing me.
25. Making me feel unnoticed or unappreciated.
26. Ignoring me.
27. Not considering me a thinking and feeling person.
28. Being too busy to care about me and listen to me.
29. Dismissing my needs as unimportant, especially when their work or hobby is more important.
30. Bringing up old mistakes from the past to deal with present problems.
31. Teasing excessively.
32. Not noticing my accomplishments.
33. Making tactless comments.
34. Liking me only for my physical looks or abilities, instead of what's inside me.

35. Not praising or appreciating me.
36. Building me up and then letting me down.
37. Getting my hopes up to do something as a family and then not following through.
38. Correcting me without reminding me that they love me.
39. Disciplining me in harshness and anger.
40. Not reasoning with me, and never giving me an explanation of why I'm being disciplined.
41. Misusing brute force.
42. Reacting to me in the opposite way I think a Christian should treat me.
43. Raising their voices to each other.
44. Not being interested in who I am.
45. Cutting down something I am doing or someone I am with as being dumb or stupid.
46. Using foul language when they are upset with me.
47. Being impatient, which often comes across as rudeness.
48. Saying "no" without giving a reason.
49. Not praising me.
50. Sensing a difference between what is said with the mouth and what is said through facial expressions.
51. Making sarcastic remarks about me.
52. Making fun of my hopes, dreams and accomplishments.
53. Punishing me severely for something I didn't do.
54. Being distracted when I really have something to say.
55. Insulting me in front of others.
56. Speaking before thinking through how it will affect me.
57. Pressuring me when I already feel low or offended.
58. Comparing me with other kids at school and telling me how wonderful they are and that I should be better.
59. Forcing me to argue with them when I'm really hurt inside.
60. Treating me like a little child.
61. Not approving of what I do or how I do it. I keep trying to get their approval but they just won't give it.
62. Seeing them do the very things they tell me not to do.

63. Ignoring me when I ask for advice because they are too busy.
64. Ignoring me and not introducing me to people who come to the house or whom we see in public.
65. Showing favoritism toward my brother or sister.
66. Acting as if something I want is of little importance.
67. Not making me feel I am special to them. It's so important to me to have my parents let me know, even in small ways, that I'm special.
68. Seeing my father put my mother down, especially in front of company.
69. Seldom touching or holding me.
70. Hearing Mom and Dad bickering at each other to the point where one of them is really hurt.
71. Not trusting me.
72. Making fun of something physically different about me.
73. My Mom and Dad trying to get revenge against each other.
74. My Dad never approving of what I do or how I do it.
75. Not being able to control their anger.
76. Getting mad at me because I can't keep up with their schedule or abilities.
77. Making me feel like they wish they had never had me in the first place.
78. Not having enough time for me.
79. Needing my parents, but they are glued to the television.
80. Seeing my parents spend a lot of money on their pleasure, but when I want something, they don't seem to have the money.
81. Making me feel childish.
82. Not spending the time to understand what I am trying to say.
83. Yelling at me when I already know I'm wrong.
84. Making me feel like I hadn't tried to improve at something when I really had.

That very lengthy list is enough to make even the best parent feel guilty! In those eighty-four items are behaviors familiar to all of us. It is striking how many of them have to do with communication between parent and child, and how many have to do with spending time with the child. It is almost as if the children whom Smalley interviewed have been reading the same books on child rearing that so many parents have been buying in recent years!

The overarching lesson in that litany of children's complaints is that we should treat children with the same respect, care, and courtesy that we treat other persons with whom we work and socialize. Good parent-child relations are not that much different from good human relations!

An obvious and helpful way to check the quality of your interaction with your child is to compare it with the way you relate to people outside the family.

When you eat with the family around the table at home, are you as patient with your child when he knocks over a glass of iced tea as you would be with a guest from the office who made the same mistake?

When you play tennis with your son as your doubles partner, and he hits a ball that belongs to you, are you as courteous to him as you would be to a friend from the country club?

When you are in the car ready to leave with your child, and he delays your departure for thirty seconds, are you as pleasant to him when he finally arrives as you would be to a neighbor?

If the answer to these questions—and a hundred more like them—is no, chances are your family relations could be improved simply by treating your children as you treat others. They deserve to be treated at least as well as the strangers you meet in the supermarket!

HUMAN RELATIONS ACTIVITY

Let's play a game!

Each day, choose a different member of your family to be
the subject of affirmation for the day. At the front door,
place a container with pencils and index cards. When
you or another family member enters, write a positive
statement about that person and place it in the container.
When the family is all together, have each family member draw a card from the container and read aloud the
positive thought.

13 "Copeability"—Critical for Success

"Copeability": the ability to cope with adversity in a way that makes the individual a stronger and better person.

All of us will experience a full share of trouble in life. Compared to the outer reaches of the universe, your journey of life is but as tall as a kitchen stepladder; compared with eternity, it is but the blink of an eye. Within this relatively short span of time, you are going to get knocked down many times. But your life will be more rewarding and productive if you can learn to accept difficulties in stride and press on.

Nothing helps children absorb the blows of life as much as a strong inner sense of self-worth. As parents, we are naturally eager to protect them from pain and problems. When they are very young we can do this in a very literal and tangible way, by protecting them from danger and watching carefully over them.

A common parental tendency, however, is to prolong this period of the child's life, never letting the child experience the normal amount of pain and difficulty so necessary to learning how to deal with it. We smooth things out for our children, taking care of as many of the hassles in advance as we possibly can so our children won't feel pressure or need. Psychologist Kevin Leman calls this "snowplowing the roads of life" for our children, and the unfortunate result, he says, is that children are never able to learn to drive the snowplow for themselves.

In addition to learning to expect good things, children must learn to respond positively when bad things happen, because adversity will definitely come to every one of us. A part of the parent's job is to teach the child the art of "copeability"—handling the hurts and failures of life with poise, and with a positive, constructive response.

Positive thinkers should actually try to respond cheerfully when hardships confront them, because hardships offer the opportunity to grow and become stronger. As the Bible tells us, "Consider yourselves fortunate when all kinds of trials come your way, because you know that when your faith succeeds in facing such trials, the result is the ability to endure."

Byron Janis was a child prodigy concert pianist, performing with the NBC Symphony Orchestra even before he was a teenager. At age fifteen he made his debut with the Pittsburgh Symphony, and he became a personal pupil of the great Vladimir Horowitz. At the age of twenty, Janis debuted at Carnegie Hall to great critical acclaim, and he came to be regarded by many experts as the world's greatest interpreter of Chopin.

It might seem that Janis, who is now a mature, middle-aged performer, just floated through life on a magic carpet of success and ease. In fact, quite the opposite is true. He has had a lifelong battle with various physical problems, and is a great pianist today only because he learned how to cope.

At age ten he ran into a glass door and lost the tendon of the little finger of his left hand. At twenty-four he was left with a painful neck problem following an auto accident. At twenty-six, he developed severe bursitis in his right shoulder and at age forty-five suffered the first signs of arthritis, his fingers growing red, swollen, and painful.

Janis became less and less capable of performing up to his high personal standards. By 1984, playing the piano at all seemed almost impossible. He stopped performing and became despondent. All his life he had been a fighter, and at the brink of total despair he made one last effort to fight back at physical disability and won. He recalls the struggle: "The first thing I had to conquer was fear. I realized what a debilitating thing fear is . . . that it can render you helpless. I know that fear breeds fear, that if you think something terrible is going to happen, it frequently does."

The catalyst for his comeback, Janis says, was the very simple realization that "I couldn't control the fact that I had arthritis, but I could control how I coped with it."

He resumed playing. His crippling disease forced him to alter his practice routine as well as some of his keyboard techniques. But by the winter of 1985, his comeback was complete, and he played in concert at the White House to a thunderous ovation. He then conducted a tour of concerts around the country to benefit the National Arthritis Foundation. Janis's bottom-line pronouncement on his situation was, "I still have arthritis. But it doesn't have me."

All of us will have temporary defeats; winners learn how to

transcend them and move on. We must prepare our children for this basic fact of life. Many famous, successful people had problems when they were young. Isaac Newton made poor grades. Walt Disney was fired because he didn't have any good ideas. Beethoven was told by his teacher that he was hopeless as a composer. Churchill flunked the fifth grade. Elvis Presley flunked an audition for his first television show. Marlon Brando played hookey from school so often that his sister had to take him to school on a leash. Bruce Springsteen was stuffed into a garbage can by one schoolteacher because she said that was where he belonged.

How do children learn to cope? Primarily through seeing their parents cope effectively. In a later chapter we will talk more about "modeling," the powerful learning pattern established between parent and child. Children learn to behave as they see their parents behave on a daily basis, and nowhere is this more evident than in learning to cope. Probably because they have seen me spend so much of my time as an administrator responding to problems and coping with them, both of my sons have shown unusual resilience and ability to bounce back from adversity.

My son Michael was born with a speech problem and a rather pronounced bowleggedness. With the help of professionals, Michael overcame these problems at an early age and today shows no signs at all that they ever existed. This child's ability to cope throughout those difficulties taught me a fresh lesson in the power of the human spirit to convert lemons into lemonade. Michael was my ever-present reminder that we were made to cope.

Psychologist James Dobson is particularly emphatic in describing the importance of helping our children cope constructively with failure and feelings of inferiority. "A sizable proportion of all human activity is devoted to the task of shielding us from the inner pain of inferiority," he writes in *Hide or Seek*. "I believe this to be the most dominant force in life, even exceeding the power of sex in its influence. Therefore, if we are to understand the meaning of behavior in our boys and girls . . . we must begin by investigating the ways human beings typically cope with self-doubts and personal inadequacies." Coming from one of America's top experts on self-esteem in children, that is strong stuff indeed.

Dobson identifies five *nonconstructive* ways in which children cope with inferiority. They are as follows: (1) withdrawal, (2) fighting, (3) denial of reality, (4) conforming, (5) becoming a clown. A better coping mechanism, he says, is the sixth common response, which he calls "compensation." This provides the healthy emotional energy for virtually every kind of human success.

Compensation is the conversion of negative energy, such as anger or pain, into a positive energy which flows toward some new, desirable goal. Finding oneself frustrated in one direction, the individual turns in an entirely different direction and allows the emotional power to fuel this new, constructive behavior.

By focusing on some new goal, the child is distracted from the pain of the negative situation. In this way, a child's natural tendency to "perseverate" (that is, to think obsessively about a thing) in regards to a failure, embarrassment, or disappointment is broken, which is necessary for true healing to occur.

It is the mechanism of compensation that is the heart of the Byron Janis story. The child learns, usually as a result of his parents' example and guidance, that the only constructive way to cope with feelings of fear and inadequacy is to aspire for compensating achievement.

Help your children learn how to cope with their problems, frustrations, and disappointments.

1. *Understand that children have a right to their feelings.*

Nothing is more futile than to tell children how to feel, or to browbeat them into denying the emotions they are honestly experiencing. If they feel bad about themselves, teach them that such a feeling is natural, but they need not wallow in it or yield to it. It is important to begin by acknowledging the feeling itself in an honest way.

2. *Set a positive example in reacting to your own frustrations.*

Although it would not be advisable to make children aware of *all* your problems, it is important for children to see you handle your hurts in a constructive manner. Obviously, this is not possible if they do not see your hurts at all. If parents hide problems from their children, the children never learn anything about a parent's own coping behavior.

If you express anger or disappointment in the presence of your children, make sure you express your ultimately positive response in their presence also. It is common for parents to express negative reactions to a problem in front of their child, then pull themselves together and cope with the problem in private, without the child's ever knowing it was eventually solved. If the child sees you blow off steam, make sure he also sees you work through the problem in a measured, reasonable manner.

3. *Find the cause of your child's frustration.*

This means listening, and some of the lessons from chapter 11 apply here. Often the child needs more than a pep talk on coping; he needs some specific advice on what he might do in a practical way. You will be unable to provide that advice if you do not understand the true underlying frustration that the child is feeling—not just the symptom of the problem, but the problem itself.

4. *Show children that a temporary failure does not affect your love for them.*

Many children are paralyzed with the fear that their parents' love for and acceptance of them is contingent on their success. We parents would not knowingly communicate that to our children, but it is often implicit in the way we relate to them. In high-achieving, success-oriented families, it is very easy for a child to feel that basic love and family support will stop if the child is not an achiever. This is one of those self-fulfilling prophecies that undermines the child's self-confidence and produces a new round of setbacks.

Somehow, parents must find ways to affirm their children even when they are misbehaving. A child needs to feel that his parents are a haven to which he can retreat when things are going badly. The parents must be seen as persons who will understand the failure, love in spite of it, and provide a base from which the child can bounce back. If the parents have so emphasized success that they are perceived as intolerant of failure, they simply add to the child's emotional burden in failure.

That fine balance comes when we applaud every success with true enthusiasm, and accept the child's failure with compassion and poise. That provides the child with a parental ally in his own attempt to cope.

To love the sinner while hating the sin is a difficult thing to do, much less communicate. To affirm the child while rejecting a particular behavior in which the child is engaging is a subtle thing to communicate, but it lies at the heart of good parenting.

"COPEABILITY" ACTIVITY

Bad things happen.
Learn to respond positively!

You might find time every other weekend to play a
challenging game. Set up a situation. You can use index
cards to present situations. Draw a card. For example,
"Your best friend is moving to Europe next week. How
will you react?" Brainstorm together ways to cope with
the situation in a positive fashion. One positive reaction
could be, "I now have a new place to visit!"

14 Team Building—Sharing Success

As an athlete and a coach, I have always understood the importance of teamwork whenever a group of people work toward a goal. Every coach worth his whistle has made pep talks and shouted slogans about the value of teamwork. When I became a parent, I found it useful to think of my family as a team, and myself as its coach. I realized that making my children into a family team could be of critical importance to the kinds of adults they became. No matter how hard I worked at being a good father, our family would not be successful if the entire team didn't work together.

Here are a few tips for making your children a part of your team:

1. *Allow your children to participate in meaningful decisions.*

131

Richard M. DeVos, president of one of the nation's leading corporations and listed personally as one of the four hundred wealthiest men in the country, is a dedicated family man who has successfully reared four children while building his company.

One of the keys to the DeVos paternal style was allowing his children, even when they were quite young, to participate in deciding where the family's philanthropic dollars would go. Periodically, he would sit down at the dining room table with his wife and four children, tell them how much money was available for charitable giving, then place before them all the requests he had received from various organizations seeking help.

The DeVos family then made decisions together, with each child, however young, jumping into the discussion to advocate his or her favorite choice. "These kids are going to grow up with money," DeVos once explained matter-of-factly, "and they may as well be learning how to use it wisely."

Not all families have this particular decision to make, but most have various important matters that might safely be submitted to a family discussion group. The choice of vacation sites, how to spend special family evenings, the type of automobile to buy, and many other decisions normally made by parents alone can often be made with full family involvement.

It is an axiom in management that people perform better in tasks that they have a hand in choosing, and a family is no different from a corporation in this sense. Children who feel they have "ownership" of the family's goals and efforts commit more enthusiastically to them.

2. *Give all members of the family as much information as possible about what is happening.*

Like any other social organization, the family thrives on information. The more aware its members are of where the unit is heading, and what is coming up next, the better they feel about being a part of it.

Unfortunately, many fathers are particularly poor in sharing goals and future plans with children, and often even with their wives. The stereotypic image of the "strong, silent type" of male leadership still prevails in many American homes, in which father gives the orders and expects the children to obey trustingly and silently.

Alan Dershowitz, the famous defense attorney and Harvard Law School professor, once said this terse form of familiar communication was best described by Ring Lardner. Lardner tells of a conversation between a son and his father while the two were driving through a maze of city streets. The boy suspected that his father might be lost but was reluctant to suggest such a thing. When finally the boy asked, "Dad, are we lost?" the father responded in classic fashion. Lardner put it this way: " 'Shut up,' he explained."

Many children, I fear, get that kind of "explanation" from their parents, especially when the family faces a particularly stressful situation. Children ask lots of questions, and answering them with patience and clarity can be tiresome, especially if the parent is under pressure. We can all identify with the father in the Ring Lardner description; if one is already lost, anxious, and irritated, the last thing needed is the persistent questioning of a youngster.

But the parent who tells children what is going on is usually the parent whose children feel they are on a team. Children can usually be trusted to understand far more than we expect them to understand. It is so easy to be condescending and to underestimate their ability.

3. *Never miss an opportunity to express pride in what your children accomplish.*

This is such an obvious point that it is easily overlooked. Parental pride and involvement are the high-octane fuel on which children run, and it is virtually impossible to give them too much of it.

To most children, the parent is the most important score-keeper. It is the parent who tells the child whether he is a winner or a loser, and it is the parent who invests the child's activities with value by showing interest in them. There are few payoffs for accomplishment more important to children than that of pleasing their parents. No athlete enjoys playing on a team whose coach is impossible to satisfy.

Lee Iacocca recalled for *Parade* magazine an element of his own boyhood motivation:

> My father and I were very close. I loved pleasing him, and he was always terrifically proud of my accomplishments. If I won a spelling contest at school, he was on top of the world. Later in life whenever I got a promotion, I'd call my father right away and he'd rush out to tell all his friends. At Ford, each time I brought out a new car, he wanted to be the first to drive it. In 1970, when I was named president of Ford Motor Company, I don't know which of us was more excited.

It is a common fear of parents that they will spoil their children if they give too much praise. It is not considered good form to dote on children excessively, and parents often fail to express the pride they genuinely feel because they fear too much approval will produce a conceited or self-centered child.

Consequently, the natural pride of many parents is held in check, never expressed, and children misread this lack of affirmation as a sign that the parents do not approve of them and their behavior. The impact on the child's self-esteem is predictably negative: "If I can't please my parents, I must not be a very worthwhile person." A parent should remember that children are praise-seeking creatures, and they will find an adult somewhere to satisfy their need for self-esteem. The parent who wants his children to feel a part of a family team will make sure that he is an adult who appreciates and praises.

4. *Don't be afraid to let your child see your own weaknesses and failures.*

Too many parents feel that they have to be superdads and supermoms in order to maintain a child's respect. To the contrary, children want to relate to their parents as flesh-and-blood human beings, not as perfect, invulnerable demi-gods of some sort. To let children see your own fears and disappointments is a part of letting them "on the team"; it is a way of saying, "I trust you so much that I don't have to be perfect around you."

When a parent tries to fake it, he rarely fools the child anyway. Most children are sensitive to the subtle signs in a parent's mood and body language that tell them all is not well. They know when a parent is anxious or fearful, and to cam-ouflage those emotions merely tells a child that he or she is not trusted to handle negative information.

This is such an important point that Paul Conn and I dis-cussed it at some length in our earlier book, *The Power of Positive Students*. Children can be exceptionally sensitive to the true feelings that underlie an adult's professed attitude. Parents who are dutifully engaged in a forced cheerfulness, when in reality they are preoccupied with their own fears and anxieties, are rarely convincing to a child. Positive thinking as a lifestyle gains credibility with children, especially as they grow older, when parents are open with them about financial difficulties, job insecurity, illness, and other challenges the family faces.

For the same reasons, it is important to let children know about the parents' own struggles and failures as teenagers and young adults. In talking with kids about their parents, I have been amazed at the number of children who have little knowledge of the humble beginnings and heroic accomplishments of their own parents. Some of the best real-life examples of winning against great odds can be found right in our own homes, and it is a shameful waste for children not to be aware of them.

A parent who overcame reverses and disappointments earlier in life should not be reluctant, through a false sense of modesty, to discuss those times with his or her children. Once we have made it through the tough times, it is tempting to consign the story of earlier struggles to the past.

Perhaps we want our children to perceive us as having always been competent, self-confident achievers. However, a child is cheated if we take that posture. He needs to know that once you were a scared kid yourself, that once you were self-conscious about your background, or your inability to keep up with the other kids in your class, or the size of your nose. When a little boy asks his father, "Were you ever scared, Daddy?" he wants the answer to be yes because he is scared himself sometimes. When a daughter asks, "Did you ever not get asked to the prom, Mother?" she hopes the answer is yes—if a woman as poised and lovely as her mother once hoped just to be asked to a dance, then maybe things will turn out well for her!

5. *Find ways to teach your children to support each other, in good times and bad times.*

We have discussed the relationship between the parents and the individual children in the family; in the "team" metaphor, that translates to the relationship between the coach and the individual players. But another important part of teamwork is the relationship of the players to one another. If a family is to be a real team, the children must learn to share one another's successes and failures. The lateral relationship among brothers and sisters is just as important as the vertical relationships between children and parents in building a strong sense of the family as a team.

In fact, there are many cases of families with ineffective parents, even abusive parents, in which the children themselves have bonded so tightly as a team that the ill effects of inattentive parenting were somewhat neutralized.

Listen again to Lee Iacocca:

> When I grew up, we started on the premise that everybody helped each other. I mean, the kids had certain roles, the father had a role, the mother had a role. It was cooperation at the basic level. People getting along is based on people respecting one another, talking openly and asking openly what your kids need, or what the parents need from the kid. But transcending all of that, more than anything else, is deeply caring for one another. Your problems are my problems, your joys are my joys. We'll share the good and the bad . . . we had many tough times. Every day was a challenge, but somehow, every day was a happy day, because you stuck together. You stick together, and it will work out.

Building this attitude in your children requires taking the time and effort for everyone in the family to know what is going on in the life of everyone else. With the full schedules and busy lives most of us lead, that does not come easily. One works at it, or it doesn't happen. It requires parental leadership, or the household fragments into the several separate lives of its members. The home can become little more than a refueling stop for a houseful of virtual strangers who know little about what the others are doing and feeling.

Parents who are team builders use mealtimes, specially designated family evenings, trips in the car, and other occasions to listen to one another. Not just to be in one another's presence, but to listen as each one tells what is happening in his or her world. This is difficult to do when the television is on, or when both teenagers have headsets with cassette tapes blasting their own music into their ears. People cannot care about one another meaningfully if they do not *know* about one another, and that does not occur through osmosis or just by living under the same roof. It happens when people take time to listen to one another, and that usually happens only when a parent takes the lead.

TEAM-BUILDING ACTIVITY

Making children a part of a family team is of critical importance to the kinds of adults that they will become.

Monthly, gather your family together. Discuss something out of the ordinary that the family can do for dinner. Involve your children in the decision-making process by encouraging them to make suggestions. As a team, everyone has a sense of "full family involvement."

15 Positive Climate—Climate for Success

Just as certain climates facilitate the growth of certain kinds of biological life, every home creates a climate, an atmosphere in which its children grow. When I speak of the climate of a home, I refer to an overall set of emotional and attitudinal conditions—most of them subtle and unspoken—that promote the development of a certain kind of child.

Positive children can and do grow up in negative home environments, and we all know of warm, loving homes that have produced a hostile, angry child. But those are the exceptions. As a rule, the climate of a home goes a long way in determining the kinds of personalities that will emerge.

Children tend to take on the characteristics of their environments, and eventually to become like those environments.

The power of this principle is beautifully expressed in the very familiar poem by Dorothy Law Nolte.

CHILDREN LEARN WHAT THEY LIVE

If a child lives with criticism,
        he learns to condemn.
If a child lives with hostility,
        he learns to fight.
If a child lives with fear,
        he learns to be apprehensive.
If a child lives with pity,
        he learns to feel sorry for himself.
If a child lives with ridicule,
        he learns to be shy.
If a child lives with jealousy,
        he learns what envy is.
If a child lives with shame,
        he learns to feel guilty.
If a child lives with encouragement,
        he learns to be confident.
If a child lives with tolerance,
        he learns to be patient.
If a child lives with praise,
        he learns to be appreciative.
If a child lives with acceptance,
        he learns to love.
If a child lives with approval,
        he learns to like himself.
If a child lives with recognition,
        he learns it is good to have a goal.
If a child lives with sharing,
        he learns about generosity.
If a child lives with honesty and fairness,
        he learns what truth and justice are.
If a child lives with security,
        he learns to have faith in himself and
        in those about him.
If a child lives with friendliness,

> he learns that the world is a nice place
> in which to live.
> If you live with serenity,
> your child will live with peace of mind.

Positive home environments do not just naturally emerge because of positive parents. The mental and emotional world of the growing child is very different from that of the adult, and it is often necessary to stop and make the conscious effort to guarantee that the conditions in the home are positive from the child's perspective.

Positive thinkers are sometimes accused of being hooked on gimmicks, little artificial devices by which they seek to "program" positive attitudes into their children. That criticism is not well founded, in my opinion. It is not sufficient merely to be positive persons; we must also find ways to pour positive attitudes into our homes, even if the techniques seem a bit forced at times.

Smiling faces on the refrigerator door, little cards and slogans around the house, positive notes inserted into the child's schoolbooks or lunch box—all these and many other such devices do add up to a brighter, more positive climate for a family.

These measures require thought, because to a certain degree they must be tailor-made for each family. Every family has its own unique personality and style, and it rarely works to simply adopt someone else's strategies for creating a positive climate; parents must *adapt* the ideas they hear and read, and be endlessly resourceful in finding ways to do so.

The result can be a home in which positive thinking is virtually a game the entire family plays, rather than another set of rules that the parents lay down. My coauthor, Paul Conn, took his family to Europe recently. Prior to the trip, he was reading a book on European travel, which cautioned the reader that overseas tourists should be prepared to be "fanatically positive" in coping with the vicissitudes of travel.

Paul liked the sound of that phrase and shared it with his children in a pre-trip pep talk. "Remember, kids," he told them, "whatever happens on this trip, we're going to always be 'fanatically positive.' " Having said that, Paul was on the spot. He is himself not naturally the most relentlessly positive person in the world, and he had challenged his children to hold him to the very high standard of being "fanatically positive."

For the entire trip, which had its usual share of frustrations and anxious moments, the Conn family used that phrase as a slogan to remind one another when someone's smile was slipping. It became almost a family joke; anyone who dared gripe or complain about anything could expect to hear just those two words—"fanatically positive!"—from the rest of the family, and it kept the need for a bright attitude on everyone's mind throughout the trip.

Many small elements of family life help contribute to a positive climate. Music played in the home or in the car should be selected with its mood-producing qualities in mind. The way members of the family dress sends signals that are part of the climate. The order—or disorder—of the various rooms in the house are part of the climate. In fact, one of the reasons that children should be taught to keep their rooms straight is that a neat room contributes to the overall healthy climate in which the child operates.

This is not to say that the house itself should have a bland sterility. A child's room should express the personality of the child, especially after children reach the age to decorate their rooms themselves. The use of posters, their own drawings, pieces of furniture, and various dresser-top doodads should be individualized expressions of the children who occupy the room. I also recommend that a great amount of latitude be allowed in decorating the room. But once the room is set up, it is important that the parent insist on its being kept straight. A chronically messy room creates the wrong climate for a child who is trying to learn to live an orderly life.

A home with absentee parents can hardly be a positive climate. Parenting takes time, lots of it, from both father and mother, and all the refrigerator stickers and slogans in the world will not substitute for the sheer presence of parents in the home on a consistent basis.

Running through the house for a few minutes each evening and shouting "I love you!" to your kids as you leave for your next appointment does not constitute positive parenting, no matter how cheery and loving and upbeat those few minutes are. The most positive thing a parent can do for a child is to *be there*, physically and emotionally.

I must confess that I did not learn that lesson easily. As a young father, I loved my two sons, but I was so driven to be a successful coach that I effectively left the parenting up to my wife, Carolyn. I was guilty of building my whole life around coaching and winning basketball and football games. I learned my lesson the hard way.

I was ambitious and wanted to provide nice things for my family. The salary of a coach and teacher didn't provide much of that, so I got a job working at the post office during the Christmas holidays one year. I worked all night long, from 11:00 P.M. to 7:00 A.M. I taught school all day, then coached basketball practice in the afternoon, went home, caught a few hours sleep, went to work again at the post office.

Obviously, I almost never saw my wife and kids, and when I did I was so exhausted it didn't matter much anyway. The absurd thing about it was that if I had been asked why I was doing all this, I would have told you, "To provide a good life for my family!"

I kept fighting a very bad cold and should have taken time off to get some rest, but I didn't want to quit working, so instead I went to a doctor and got a big dose of penicillin so I could keep going. At work that night, I started to break out in big hives all over my body. My face, neck, and arms began to swell, and I was suddenly in severe pain, but I finished my shift.

At seven that morning, I went home and collapsed. For the first time, I physically could not go to school. I called the doctor, who told me to get to the hospital immediately. There they pumped me full of more medication. The condition simply worsened.

After two weeks in the hospital, I still was no better. The doctors were very concerned and said they needed to inject a drug into my bloodstream to kill the penicillin mold, the source of the problem. The treatment was dangerous, but we decided to proceed.

Before the treatment began, I wanted to see my two small boys. Carolyn dressed them up, brought them to the hospital parking lot, and held them up so I could see and wave to them from my window.

Looking at those two boys, I suddenly realized that I loved two little boys with all my heart. I had let my job so completely dominate my life that I barely knew them. I knew that my priorities were totally messed up, and if I got out of that hospital I was going to change things.

The treatment was successful, and I was able to go home. But I had made a decision in that hospital about the priorities in my life, and I have been a different man since.

My priorities are simple. First comes my family, *then* my job. That order was backwards in my life for many years, and it took a hard lesson to show me that. But the thing about a hardheaded Alabaman is that when he finally learns a lesson, he learns it well, and I have absolutely no difficulty remembering that being a good parent and grandparent is my most important role.

Because I want to be a good father and grandfather, I am continuously looking for ideas to use personally, and to share with my sons, Billy and Michael, and with my daughter-in-law, Janey, in building a positive climate. I want my beautiful granddaughter, Michelle, to have a positive climate in our homes as she prepares for her journey through life.

Research clearly indicates that the home environment is the most powerful factor in determining a child's success in school. I share with you, as I have with my family, characteristics of homes with positive climates which I consider most important:

- There is an emphasis on building the self-worth and self-respect of each family member.
- Each family member respects the needs, dignity, and individuality of every other family member.
- Family relationships are characterized by loving, caring, trust, and affection.
- The family unit is secure and cohesive, with pride in its members and their accomplishments. There is a feeling of ownership and opportunities for involvement and participation in family affairs.
- Fault-finding, bickering, and quarreling are kept to a minimum. Differences are settled reasonably, fairly, and amicably.
- Expectations for each family member are high, and there is cooperative effort to help each one achieve his or her goals.
- Communications are free and open. Family members are encouraged to express opinions and feelings without fear of recrimination or reprisal.

• A clearly identifiable code of values and ethics guides the decisions and behavior of each family member and of the family as a unit.

POSITIVE CLIMATE ACTIVITY

Your positive home enhances self-love!

Have each member of the family come up with a positive, catchy saying and create a picture to match it. Hang them on the doors!

---

16 Conditioning—Habits of Success

One of the responsibilities of positive parents is to see that their children are exposed to positive mental conditioning.

When the word *conditioning* is used, we immediately think of Pavlov's dogs, or perhaps of dark tales of brainwashing and mind-control techniques. Actually, conditioning is the most basic form of learning, and psychologists have studied it for over a hundred years, going back, indeed, to those famous experiments of Ivan Pavlov in which dogs were conditioned to salivate when they heard the sound of a ringing bell.

Conditioning is a very simple process, and it goes on all the time, shaping the lives of all of us, whether we realize it or not. It is a very natural process, a built-in part of the way human and animal bodies function.

147

There are two major types of conditioning, both of which affect human behavior and both of which are at work in the attitudes of our children. They are *classical* conditioning and *operant* conditioning. In both types the critical element of conditioning is the combination of two elements in the experience of the person. In any conditioning event, two things become interlocked so that one is afterwards associated with the other.

In *classical* conditioning, the combination that occurs is between any particular stimulus and another stimulus. In the case of Pavlov's famous dogs, meat powder was sprayed into the mouth of a hungry dog. Naturally, the dog salivated— that's what hungry dogs do automatically when they taste food. But Pavlov rang a bell at the same time the meat powder was presented. He did this over and over again. Every time the dog was fed, a bell rang. After this had gone on for some time, Pavlov merely rang the bell, and the dog began to salivate.

What had occurred was *classical* conditioning. One stimulus (the delivery of food) had been combined with another stimulus (a ringing bell) so often that the two were interlocked in the experience of the dog. Now the ringing of the bell caused the dog to do the same thing that only the food had done—that is, to salivate.

The interesting thing to remember is that before the conditioning, the ringing of a bell had no meaning whatever for that dog. It was just another sound. But after the conditioning occurred, bell ringing by itself was sufficient to trigger salivation, without the dog's being aware of what was going on!

Pavlov and hundreds of other experimenters since that time have shown that the same process occurs with human beings: sights, sounds, words, and all sorts of stimuli (like the bell) gain the power to make us do certain things (like salivate) as a result of being presented to us over and over again. Understanding this process, and how it affects our feelings about things, is valuable to us as individuals and as parents.

Let us start with the very simple idea that praise makes children feel good. In the language of classical conditioning, praise is the meat powder, and feeling good is salivating. The two naturally go together. If some other stimulus is repeatedly combined with praise, then eventually that stimulus alone will make the person feel good. So if the classroom at school is a place in which praise is frequently delivered, then eventually that classroom is likely to become a place where the child feels good. He doesn't usually know *why* he feels good there; he will simply describe it by saying that he "likes that class." Children are not particularly analytical about what makes them feel good and what doesn't.

What children do is try to avoid those places where they do not feel good. If the classroom is an aversive place for them, they respond by avoiding or withdrawing from the place itself, because the place is associated with bad feelings. Obviously, children cannot choose *not to go* to school; they cannot literally avoid being in the classroom. So instead, they withdraw emotionally and mentally; they "tune out." They are forced to attend physically, but they become uninvolved mentally and attitudinally.

Simple classical conditioning—it is the power of classical conditioning that makes the parent such a dominant figure in the child's life to begin with. In the earlier days and months of life, the presence of the parent is constantly associated with delivery of food, warmth, release from the irritation of wet diapers, and all sorts of other positive feelings.

The other major type of conditioning was discovered primarily by a Harvard psychologist named B. F. Skinner. Skinner called this type *operant* conditioning because he said it described the way in which the person "operates" in the world in which he lives.

The principle of operant conditioning is that all those behaviors that are followed by rewards tend to occur again, and those that are followed by punishment tend not to occur again. It is the old principle of the carrot and the stick. The mule will walk forward in order to eat the carrot (reward) or in order to avoid the stick (punishment).

Long before Skinner did his research—for thousands of years, in fact—men and women have intuitively understood the principle of reward and punishment. There is nothing new about that. What Skinner did was to give us a clearer picture of exactly how these two incentive systems work, and to offer a comparison of the two.

A child will behave in a certain way to get a candy bar, or he will behave in the same way to avoid being spanked. Both types of incentives "work," in the sense that they will elicit the desired behavior from the child. But Skinner and his colleagues have demonstrated that there are significant differences in the long-term implications of whichever incentive system is used.

Punishment has some advantages over reward. The chief advantage is that it is usually faster. It produces an immediate, clear result. If a child is told that his hand will be cut off if he reaches for another biscuit, and he believes it really will be, biscuit grabbing will be sharply and suddenly reduced! That is the major advantage of punishment over reward as a behavioral management technique.

There are several disadvantages of the frequent use of punishment, however: (1) its effect is often short-lived; (2) it reduces the overall amount of activity of the child; and (3) it elicits hostility and aggression.

First, when a child behaves in a certain way in order to avoid punishment, someone must always be present with the ability to punish. If a child gets out of bed on time in the morning only to avoid being dragged out bodily by Mother, that works fine as long as Mother is present. But what happens when Mother is not present? The child reverts to sleeping late. On the other hand, a child who gets out of bed on time in order to gain some reward is much more likely to continue arising on time when that reward is missing.

Why is reward-motivated behavior more permanent than punishment-motivated behavior? No one has ever answered that question satisfactorily, but it does seem clear that children who are taught to do things in search of reward persist in those behaviors longer, even after the immediate prospect of the reward is no longer available.

Second, children who are frequently punished tend to develop an overall behavior pattern that is less active and spontaneous. It appears that there is a tendency for punishment to spread from the undesirable behavior that one is trying to eliminate to other behaviors as well. If the child is constantly punished for various types of bad behavior, he tends to reduce the amount of bad behavior and good behavior alike. What you get is a person who does nothing, for fear of doing the wrong thing.

An example of the damaging effect of too much punishment is seen in the classroom of a teacher who responds in a negative or punishing way to students' questions when those questions happen to be poor ones. The teacher is attempting to punish the asking of an inappropriate question by embarrassing the student or responding in a way that makes the student stop asking "dumb" questions.

The treatment works. Too well. The student quits asking bad questions, but unfortunately he stops asking good questions too, simply because he cannot be sure whether the question is a good one or not a good one, and his top priority is to avoid punishment. The teacher rubs out the undesirable behavior but also rubs out the desirable behavior. Mark Twain put it this way: "A cat, having sat on a hot stove lid, will never again sit on a hot stove lid—nor on a *cold* stove lid!"

Third, excessive use of punishment produces individuals who are more likely to be hostile and aggressive than those whose behavior is managed primarily by reward. Even in laboratory mice, researchers have found that frequent use of electric shock in experiments tends to elicit from the mice a higher level of aggressive behavior, which the mice typically direct at one another.

This is another of those findings for which no one has a final explanation, but it is clear that this relationship between punishment and hostility is present also in children. When a child's behavior is managed by use of large doses of punishment from adults, the child cannot respond by directing the resulting hostility toward the adults themselves, so it is often turned in some other direction.

This is the old "kick-the-dog" syndrome, in which the executive who is upbraided by his superior at the office has no choice but to grin and bear it, until he gets home, where he takes it out on the dog—or maybe the kids! The basic point here is that punishment elicits hostility, which is sure to express itself somewhere along the line.

The effective parent will undoubtedly utilize both reward and punishment in the conditioning that takes place in the home. Both work, and each is appropriate under certain circumstances. But there are definite long-term advantages to the greater use of reward, especially if one wishes to create a climate of warmth and mutual regard while still managing the child's behavior on a daily basis.

Listed below are some suggestions that can help your children acquire the habits of success.

Power of Suggestion
- Start the day off with a quiet time with your children, and discuss positive events and happenings.
- Place positive thoughts in your children's minds daily by using "uplifting language."
- Provide positive books and music for your children to read and listen to frequently.
- Clip interesting newspaper articles to share and discuss with the children.
- Greet your children at the door enthusiastically upon their return home from school.
- Be a "Goodfinder" every day. Constantly look for the strengths and good characteristics in your children.
- Use the "whisper method"—parents whisper positive suggestions into the ears of sleeping children.

Power of Self-Suggestion (Self-Talk)
- Encourage your children to get into the habit of talking positively rather than negatively to themselves.
- Get children to affirm positive thoughts such as:

> I will make it work!
> This is my day!
> I get excited just thinking about it!
> I can do it!
> I'm terrific!

- Inform your children that most self-talk generally used, as much as 90 percent, is self-defeating. It mostly goes unnoticed; you really are not aware that you're doing it. Some examples of negative self-talk are:

> Things just never seem to go right for me.
> This just isn't my day.
> I'm sick and tired of thinking about it.

I just can't do it.
I'm no good . . . period.

Self-talk becomes a self-generating habit. Teach your children that what "I say to me" really counts. Make it positive!

Habits
- Make positive suggestions to yourself and others. These result in good habits.
- Practice, drill, and repeat positive suggestions and self-talk—they make us what we are.

CONDITIONING ACTIVITY

Change your attitude with the power of suggestion!

As a family, brainstorm positive personal statements and thoughts. Write down as many as you can think of. For example, "I am somebody special," "I believe in me," "I can do it." Whenever someone in your family chooses a negative, ZAP him or her with a positive from your list.

17 Modeling—Examples of Success

The late Lawrence Kohlberg, famous Harvard psychologist who studied moral development in children, was fond of saying that values are *"caught, not taught."* By that, he meant that children are more likely to absorb their parents' values by being around them constantly than to adopt those values through some intellectual process of logic and reasoning.

For the children who live with us day in and day out, what we do speaks more loudly than what we say. We are constantly teaching them, for better or worse, simply by being.

It is pointless to tell our children to be positive if they see us being constantly negative; it is pointless to tell them to play fair if they see us cheat; it does no good at all to lecture them about courtesy if we are habitually rude in their presence.

The process by which children become what they see is called *modeling*. Modeling is a potent learning tool that goes far beyond simple imitation itself. Imitation is a conscious process by which a person intentionally copies the behavior of someone else. Modeling, on the other hand, takes place unconsciously, as one individual gradually takes on the characteristics of someone else, particularly someone whom he likes or admires.

Modeling is one of the most common types of learning among young children; much of the growing child's everyday learning occurs as he "catches" the behavior and attitudes of adults who are prominent in his environment. The process of modeling occurs so naturally and automatically that many psychologists believe it is even more important than heredity in explaining why people within the same families are often highly similar to one another. If someone speaks of "getting my hot temper from my father," or explains his shyness with "I take after my mother," chances are strong that the trait was indeed acquired by modeling.

What is the best way to predict a child's tendency to have positive or negative attitudes? By looking at the important adults in that child's life, especially his parents. Children develop their self-esteem by observing their parents' own self-evaluations. Parents with high self-esteem tend to have children with high self-esteem, because their own ability to feel good about themselves is unconsciously modeled by the child. Parents or teachers can lecture children endlessly about the need for self-confidence, but if those adults do not exhibit a positive self-concept, the words are largely wasted.

When I was coaching, I often cautioned my athletes about the health problems associated with smoking cigarettes. One Sunday morning, as I was leaving my church after a Sunday School session, a lady came up to me and said,

"Coach Mitchell, congratulations on winning the football game last Friday night." I thanked her.

"Something has been on my mind," she went on, "that I'm going to be so bold as to ask you about. I was sitting in the stands with several other ladies and a couple of them said they thought they saw you smoking on the sidelines. I told them they must be mistaken, that Coach Mitchell would never smoke, particularly in front of his athletes, because he didn't allow his athletes to smoke or drink. I've even heard you talk about it in speeches. So I just want to know, did these ladies see you smoking or were they mistaken?"

I told her that they might be right, that I probably had smoked a cigarette or two that particular evening, even though I smoked very little.

"Are you disappointed in me because that was true?" I asked her.

"Well, to tell the truth, I would have to say yes," she replied. That got to me a little bit, and I heard myself say to her, "Let me tell you *this* . . . if it means that much to you, smoking is not that important to me, and I can assure you I'll never touch another cigarette."

After church that morning, I got in my car and started home. I opened the glove compartment, pulled out a pack of cigarettes, and threw them away. I have never touched a cigarette since.

The damage I was doing to my own body by smoking was something I had been able to justify, but somehow I couldn't tolerate the sudden awareness that these young athletes were modeling a habit that could literally kill them. It was one of those times when one suddenly knows what one must do, and I have been grateful to that woman ever since for providing me the incentive to break the habit.

I have a friend in Tennessee who became convinced that

wearing seat belts was a good idea—for his kids. He had seen one of those traffic safety films that showed how dangerous it was to be unbelted in an accident, so like a good father he began insisting that his children wear seat belts. For some reason, they never seemed to get the point. He had to remind them, every time they got into the car, to buckle up.

One day his wife pointed out to him that it might speed the learning process if he buckled his own seat belt occasionally! Rather reluctantly, he began to do so—not so much for his own sake but to set a good example for his children, and almost like magic they began to use them, too. Many months of prodding them had failed, but after a few weeks of modeling the behavior, buckling up was almost second nature to them.

I was coming from Phoenix by plane one day and was sitting across the aisle from a mother and her two young daughters. We had a hard landing as we arrived in Atlanta; the plane hit the concrete runway with a jolt. The mother started cursing the pilot, muttering loudly that he needed to go back to flight school and learn to fly.

As the airplane door opened, and we began filing off, the pilot was standing near the exit, wishing the departing passengers a good day. As the lady reached him, she flew into another tirade, telling him what a poor pilot he was. And believe it or not, her two little daughters began to chime in, loudly berating this middle-aged professional for his incompetence.

I smiled at the pilot and told him I enjoyed the flight, and left the airplane with the shrill sounds of that family still assaulting him. *What a great example of negative modeling*, I thought, and how predictably sour those kids' outlook on life will be. If the mother had laughed and made a little joke about the bumpy landing, the daughters would have undoubtedly done the same. Instead, she showed them quite a different response, and like little sponges they were picking it up.

Developmental psychologists have specified several conditions that make modeling more likely to occur, and that make it more powerful and permanent in the experience of the child: (1) the degree of similarity the child perceives between him and the model, (2) the overall level of competence and skill the model demonstrates to the child, and (3) the amount of time spent in the presence of the model.

How perfectly the parent fits in with each of these three conditions! The child sees the parent as being very *similar* to himself, having the same last name, sharing the same home and experiences; the child perceives the parent as extremely *competent*, as a powerful and all-knowing figure, especially in the very early stages of his life; the child is exposed to the parent over a long period of *time*, in a variety of circumstances and settings.

The ramifications of this are awesome: the parent is a far more potent model than any other adult in the child's social environment; and the modeling effect operates so powerfully, so quietly, and so universally that the parent is hardly aware of it—and the child is not aware of it at all. The question for parents is not whether or not to be models—they *are* models, like it or not. The question is, What kinds of models they will be?

Children absorb what they see and experience in the presence of their parents. One of the cheerful things about modeling is that it enables us to teach a positive lifestyle even when we do not fully understand ourselves how the principle works.

Have you ever pondered the fact that millions of people have done quite an effective parenting job without ever reading a book like this one, or without having studied any of the concepts of parenting? Intuitively, without thinking about what they were doing, they simply produced terrific, positive children.

This is true, of course, because one need *not* understand modeling to do it. One need not read a book about how to teach kids to be honest; one need only behave honestly oneself to model that trait and hence teach it on a daily basis. Some very important reminders can help you become a more positive role model:

1. You are sending ongoing messages to your children which communicate your attitudes, skills, and knowledge.

2. We send several hundred verbal and nonverbal messages to our children each day.

3. Silence speaks. You do not have to say one word to send a message to your child. You can turn off verbal communication but not nonverbal.

4. The learning of nonverbal communication begins shortly after birth and is practiced and refined throughout life. An infant communicates nonverbally with the parent before it can speak.

5. Research suggests that only 7 percent of a message is sent through verbal communication; the remaining 93 percent is sent through body language and vocal intonation.

6. "Winning words" should be used in talking with your children, never any "put-down" language.

7. Your *words* and your *deeds* should signal the same message—in other words, we must practice what we preach.

MODELING ACTIVITY

Action speaks louder than words!

Take some positives that you have generated and from them create mini-posters, pictures, and sayings. Shower them all over your home. Take it even one step further. As a family, make some for friends and loved ones, especially those who may be experiencing rough moments in their lives.

18 Positive Reinforcement— Encouraging Success

We are all familiar with the experiment of the rat in the maze, seeking a piece of cheese. A rat is placed at one end of a maze, the cheese at the other. The food acts as a magnet, drawing the rat through the maze. The rat learns the design of the maze almost incidentally, as the animal searches for the food. The point of the whole exercise, from the rat's point of view, is not to learn the maze but to get to the cheese. Maze learning is a by-product of food getting.

In psychological terms the cheese at the end of the maze is the *positive reinforcement*, and many behavioral scientists will tell us that there is some symbolic version of that cheese underlying virtually all types of learning. Even for human beings, learning occurs as a by-product of our constant search for certain amenities we want in our lives, things that are usually less tangible than cheese. And among the most powerful of reinforcements is praise or other personal expressions of appreciation and encouragement.

With children, positive reinforcement takes many forms—a smile, an approving nod or pat on the back, praise for correct answers rather than disapproval for wrong ones, appreciation for projects or chores well done, notes of encouragement, and reassurances of affection. The only limit to the types of positive reinforcement is the imagination of the adult. In my work with the POPS Foundation, I saw again and again the need for both a lifestyle and a work style of positive reinforcement in our educational systems.

I gave the keynote address one morning at a meeting of school administrators and that evening spoke to parents and patrons in the school district. At the conclusion of the meeting with parents, a lady came up to me, reached for my hand, and told me she had something important to share with me. With tears streaming down her face, she said, "Dr. Mitchell, I am not a parent and I do not have any children in school. I came here tonight to share with you something that happened after your address to our school administrators. I work in the district office. My boss came by my office after the session and told me he appreciated me and thanked me for what I did for him. Looking at him, I said, 'Do you realize this is the first time in the twenty-six years I have been working here that anyone has ever said that to me!' "

The woman continued, "I just wanted to share that information with you and let you know how touched I was by his words. Just because I was being paid to do my job, he had thought that was sufficient. We all need to be reinforced and told we are appreciated."

Even in a workplace populated by professional educators,

the simple power of positive reinforcement had been over-looked. Twenty-six years is a long time to work without a thank-you, but that is more common, I fear, than one might think. Take that condition and spread it over twelve years of elementary and secondary school, and it is little wonder that our young people lack positive self-regard.

A young man once told me of his experience on the staff of a large church in Florida. He had worked for over two years under the direct supervision of the pastor, surviving several mini-crises on the job along the way. He often wondered if he was meeting the pastor's expectations and would occasionally ask, only to receive a rather taciturn "Okay." The young man grew increasingly plagued by a fear that he was not perform-ing well and became increasingly frustrated by the lack of feedback. No matter how many apparent successes, the pas-tor never mentioned his work one way or another. He was convinced he must be doing something to displease his boss and became discouraged almost to the point of resigning.

Finally he could handle the situation no longer, so he made an appointment with the pastor, sat down in his office, and asked him in a direct fashion, "I have been working here over two years. You have never told me whether my work is good, bad, or indifferent. I must be doing something wrong, but I don't know what it is, so will you please tell me. If it's some-thing I can correct, I will, and if not, I'll quit."

The pastor seemed genuinely startled by the young man's outburst. "I think you're doing terrific work," he responded. "You're making an excellent contribution in a tough job, and I don't know how I would replace you. Don't even *think* about leaving!"

The young man was amazed at the warmth and sincerity of the praise. "Well, if you think I'm doing well, why haven't you ever told me?" he asked. And the pastor answered, "If you foul up, I'll let you know. If I don't say anything at all, it means you're doing fine."

The young man did not resign. He resumed his work with higher self-esteem and probably a corresponding increase in productivity. Unfortunately, the pastor's response was what is often a common management attitude: consider the absence of punishment to be the equivalent of praise. The problem is that we human beings don't operate that way. We run on positive reinforcement the way automobiles run on gasoline. If the cheese is not available, the rat loses interest in running through the maze. Employees who threaten to resign often do so in an attempt to elicit from their supervisors the praise they cannot get any other way.

Failure to deliver positive reinforcement is one kind of problem in the workplace, an even more serious one when it occurs in the home. Adults can create their own self-reinforcers when others do not deliver them, but children are not as adept at self-motivation, and often have fewer resources. For some children, the home is all there is, and the parents are often the only source of positive reinforcement. They need it like a fragile plant needs water.

Robert E. Fisher, in *The Language of Love*, says:

> Nothing builds self-esteem in others like honest praise and appreciation. If we want our family members to feel good about themselves we need to be . . . lavish in our praise. There is good reason why we love to have those dogs around who are always wagging their tails. Their behavior says, "I like you. You are my best friend." How much more meaningful is it to have a fellow human being say by his actions and by his words, "I love you and appreciate you. You are a worthwhile person." It is tragic that so many people *never* receive such messages, even from those closest to them. To compound the tragedy, usually those persons receive instead a constant barrage of criticism and

accusation. Is it any wonder we have so many people in our society bound by feelings of inferiority, guilt, and insecurity?

In our humanistic world we are told the only way to rid ourselves of our negative feelings and troubles is to tap our inner resources—to pull ourselves up by our own bootstraps—to become "self-actualized." The implication is that we should not expect nor do we need any "outside" help. There are two basic things we need to understand about that philosophy: It is wrong and it does not work.

When Blanchard and Spencer's *One-Minute Manager* was first released, it had a dramatic impact in the American corporate community, partially because its advice to managers was so fresh and had so much face validity. But the core principle in the book is actually little more than this basic principle of positive reinforcement, freshly presented this way: "Be a Goodfinder. Find someone doing something good and praise it." A "goodfinder" is simply a person who delivers positive reinforcement.

In the POPS program in public schools, we borrowed the "goodfinder" concept and heard many testimonials of how it changed the behavior of veteran professional educators. A teacher in West Virginia remarked to me that she had a principal who was the most negative person in the world. He had a keen eye for the worst in people and seemed blind to the good. After the "Be a Goodfinder" slogan was emphasized in his school, he began to write notes to teachers and parents expressing positive personal things to them.

According to the teacher, the entire faculty began to mirror the principal's behavior. While the principal had been negative, the teachers were negative. When the principal became positive, teachers found themselves striving to change their own behavior. In turn, the teachers' influence on the children became positive, and the school began to have fewer discipline problems, fewer suspensions, and more students making the honor roll.

I was reminded recently how easy it is, even for those of us who know better, to neglect "goodfinding" right in our own homes. For many years, I have been in the habit of getting up early in the morning, going for a good fast run around the neighborhood for exercise, going home for a shower and change of clothes, then sitting down for breakfast before going to work.

My favorite breakfast is good homemade biscuits and milk gravy, Southern style. My wife Carolyn bakes the best biscuits in the world; I have been enjoying her delicious biscuits every morning for years. One morning, I sat down to breakfast and noticed that instead of biscuits there was toast on my plate. Carolyn had put a toaster right on the table and had made whole wheat toast instead of my usual biscuits and gravy.

I assumed that she didn't have the ingredients she needed to make biscuits that morning, and I didn't think much more about it. But the next morning I was served whole wheat toast again, and this continued for several days. After about a week of this, I asked Carolyn if she would like me to go to the store and buy the ingredients she needed to make biscuits.

"I have what I need for biscuits," she said. "I just thought I would make toast instead."

"Why?" I asked in an aggrieved voice. "You know how much I enjoy biscuits and gravy."

"Well, no," said Carolyn, "I actually didn't know you cared about my biscuits, one way or another, since you never said anything."

I got the message and spent the next few minutes telling her in some detail how much her biscuits meant to me. The next morning, I came in from running, took my shower, and there on the breakfast table were biscuits and gravy again!

This time I didn't miss my cue. "Hey, thanks for these biscuits," I exclaimed. "Wow, these are really great!" And I meant every word of it. She had reminded me not to take for granted the need for positive reinforcement right there in my own home. I have never failed since to let her know how much I appreciate those biscuits.

Here are some ways to use positive reinforcement in preparing your children for a successful and confident journey through life.

1. *Praise*

Recognizing and praising positive behavior improves the likelihood of repetition. (Ignore negative behavior unless it is harming the child or others.) Avoid correcting your children by using negative verbal expressions; this causes children to become resentful and negative. Express approval or admiration for positive behavior both verbally (I like that) and nonverbally (a wink or a touch on the arm).

To use praise most effectively:

- Be specific—Be specific in detailing exactly what behavior is being praised. For example, your child is playing with a friend in a proper manner. Instead of, "You're a good girl, Michele," say, "Michele, I appreciate and like the way you're playing with your friend today."
- Be sincere—Build feelings of trust and acceptance with sincere verbal or nonverbal praise.
- Be prompt—Praise immediately after a deed.
- Be fair—Base praise on what it is possible for each child to achieve, and avoid comparing one child with another. It is very important that parents praise and recognize children for themselves alone.

To use praise as a means of positive reinforcement:

- Give children a specific task and then praise them for completing it.
- Display their schoolwork on the refrigerator door.
- Praise them in the presence of the entire family, such as at the dinner table.

Teach your children to accept praise graciously by saying thank you.

2. *Encouragement*

It is the art of "turning your children on," helping them to do for themselves, not doing for them.

Factors conducive to encouragement:

- Acceptance of children as they are.
- Confidence shown in them.
- A nonblaming attitude.
- Empathy.
- A nonjudgmental attitude.

To use encouragement as a means of positive reinforcement:

- Assign chores to children. Give assistance only as needed.
- Encourage children to express their views and opinions.
- Ask children to share with family members what they did at school.
- Teach your children to write thank-you notes to others.
- Stress to your children the importance of asking questions when necessary.

Language of encouragement:

- "I like the way you handled that."
- "How do you feel about it?"

- "You'll make it."
- "I have confidence in your judgment."
- "Thanks, that helped a lot."
- "It was very thoughtful of you to wash the dishes."
- "You may not feel you've reached your goal, but look how far you have come."
- "It looks as if you have really spent a lot of time thinking that through. Sounds great to me."

Characteristics of encouraging parents:

- See children as individuals.
- Are enthusiastic.
- Feel great about themselves.
- Eliminate negative expectations.
- Provide children with positive feedback.
- Recognize effort.
- Care.
- Trust.
- Smile.
- Avoid double standards.
- Uplift their children daily.

Parents must have a systematic plan for using encouragement so that it becomes a habit.

3. *Affection*

Affection is important to the normal physical and emotional development of children. Recent studies have shown that premature babies who were soothed, massaged, and touched by nurses in hospitals gained more weight and matured to a point at which they could go home much sooner than babies who did not receive affection and touching. Telling your children that you love them is important. However, it is more important to show that you love your children through physical expressions such as touching, hugging, and kissing. It is also important to express your love and affection in other ways. Such expressions may seem insignificant, but their impact is powerful.

- Send cards on your children's birthdays.
- Leave little notes saying "I love you" or "You're special."
- Call them personally on the phone.
- Surprise them with little gifts, trips to the zoo, and the like.
- Make their favorite dessert.

4. *Appreciation*

Children need and want simple appreciation and approval from their parents and others who are important to them. A way of providing appreciation is through positive words and compliments. Both are priceless. Mark Twain once remarked that he could live for two months on a compliment. Show your appreciation in many ways to your children. One of the best ways of expressing appreciation is simply by saying, "Thank you" and "I appreciate you." Expressing your appreciation to your family members just as you do to colleagues at work or to your closest friends is extremely important.

5. *Smiles*

The memory of a smile *can last forever*.

- Children are enriched by smiles.
- Smiles create happiness in the home.
- Smiles are sunshine to discouraged children.
- Smiles are the best antidote for children in trouble.
- Remember! Children who feel they do not have reasons to smile need your smiles frequently.

POSITIVE REINFORCEMENT ACTIVITY

Be a "Goodfinder"!

See how many times in a day you can catch your children being good. Immediately tell them how proud you are of their positive behavior. Share with other family members how you caught that member of your family being good today.

19 Determination—Determinant of Success

Even as a youngster, Lou Holtz wanted to be around Notre Dame. He dreamed of becoming the coach of Notre Dame. In high school he just made the 103 pounds needed to wrestle. And he graduated 234th in a class of 278. And the image of the consummate football coach? He measures five feet ten inches and weighs 150 pounds.

But he overcame adversity. He played college football, and he was graduated from Kent State and took his master's from Iowa. "Show me anyone who is successful and I'll show you someone who has overcome adversity." Today he is one of the nation's outstanding coaches and motivational speakers.

Coach Holtz served as assistant coach at the University of Connecticut, University of South Carolina, Ohio State, and

William and Mary. He was head coach of the New York Jets. He is a motivator par excellence, and has a career record of 141 wins, 75 losses, and 5 ties. He won the national collegiate title in his third season at Notre Dame. His own achievements he attributes in large part to positive thinking. He dreamed of succeeding, he determined to succeed, and he accomplished what he set out to do.

The chief determinant of success is not IQ, but personal determination—the attitude that "I can, I will!"

Determination is an inner resource more important than any single set of skills, talents, or advantages. When speaking to groups of young people, I like to compare mental attitudes to the battery of an automobile, a common object which even elementary school children can understand.

If you have ever lived in the north, you know what happens to cars when the mercury drops; severely cold weather affects the battery. In some cases, the battery becomes so weak that the car has to be started with jumper cables, that is, with assistance from an outside source. In the same way one's family and social environments can weaken the spirit of determination, corroding it with negative thoughts. To become productive, such a person needs outside help; he needs the strength provided by a positive rather than a negative climate.

On the other hand, some car batteries are stronger than others. Even in the coldest weather they respond instantly to a turn of the ignition key. Likewise with the human spirit. Even when exposed to the most extreme negative conditions, some people have the inner strength to exercise amazing determination and achieve amazing success.

To illustrate the dramatic way in which determination can overcome other circumstances, consider three brief profiles, all of them true. In each case the young person described could be expected to wind up a neurotic, delinquent, or even psychotic adult.

1. A girl, age sixteen, had become parentless, assigned to the custody of a grandmother because her mother, who was separated from an alcoholic husband, rejected the child as being homely, a liar, and one who stole sweets. The father, before dying from alcoholism, had been fond of the girl, and she lived a fantasy as the mistress of his household.

Living with her grandmother, the girl was part of a household that included four uncles and aunts. One of the uncles had a drinking problem and left home as a result. One aunt was so emotionally affected by a love affair that she often locked herself in a room for days at a time. The grandmother, feeling she had failed with her own children, became unreasonably strict with the girl, dressing her in odd-looking clothes, refusing to let her have playmates or to even attend school, and putting her in a brace in a misguided attempt to guarantee that she would develop good posture. By age sixteen, she seemed destined to failure and maladjustment.

2. A boy in his senior year of high school obtained a certificate from a physician stating that a nervous breakdown made it necessary for him to leave school for six months. He was a poor student, whom teachers regarded as a problem. He had no friends. His father died while the boy was young, having made clear his disappointment in the son because he lacked athletic ability. The boy had many odd mannerisms, including making up his own religion and chanting hymns to himself. Such a child's chances for success seemed remote.

3. A boy, age six, was born with a large head and was thought to have brain damage. Relatives and neighbors agreed that he was abnormal in some way, though his father regarded him as merely stupid. His mother, however, insisted on sending him to school, where a teacher diagnosed him as

mentally ill, forcing the mother to withdraw him from school and teach him herself. At home his behavior included such bizarre episodes as setting fire to the barn and smashing eggs by sitting on them in an effort to hatch them.

These are three examples of young people with very little likelihood of being productive, much less highly successful, as adults. But that was not the case.

The unwanted sixteen-year-old ugly duckling who was not allowed to have friends or attend school was Eleanor Roosevelt.

And the poor student with the odd mannerisms? He was Albert Einstein.

The boy who thought he could hatch eggs, whose father labeled him stupid? That was Thomas Alva Edison!

All three of these persons were, for different reasons, thought to be poorly equipped for success in adult life, yet went on to make an extraordinary impact on the generations in which they lived. Although each exhibited a certain kind of genius, none was tested as having a genius-level IQ.

All of them, however, displayed amazing degrees of determination. It was Edison who said that genius is 1 percent inspiration and 99 percent perspiration. Despite horrendous negative influences, they developed positive attitudes, gained belief in their own abilities, and built a self-confidence that did not crumble in the face of temporary failures. Each is a marvelous example of the fact that it is not IQ but "I can, I will" that matters most.

Dr. Benjamin Bloom, noted professor of education at the University of Chicago, conducted a study of 120 top American artists, athletes, and scholars. He found the secret to success of the outstanding persons was Drive and Determination—not natural talent. The five-year study looked at Olympic swimmers, tennis players, pianists, sculptors, mathematicians, and research neurologists. *In almost every instance, hard work along with parental support was the determinant of success.*

The mathematicians, it was found, were rarely at the top of their class as youngsters. By the age of fourteen, they were studying twenty-four hours a week, the time most kids spend watching television.

Parents of these 120 achievers who were studied were not outstanding in their children's fields. They merely exposed their children to those fields. Then they and other family members provided strong encouragement—while caring teachers and coaches played their important roles in nurturing the children's basic talents. Success did not occur at a snap of the fingers. Rather, in every case, success resulted from a long, step-by-step development.

There is no question that positive parental guidance and teacher-coach encouragement greatly affect a youngster's ability to succeed. Conversely, I believe the lack of such guidance and encouragement impedes greatly a youngster's development.

Too many young people—and parents and teachers as well—have allowed IQ labels to set artificially low limits on what they expect to achieve. There is a tendency to invest far too much of one's self-evaluation in a test score that is often badly flawed and misleading. At best an IQ score is merely a measurement of one's ability to think and reason. It is not a measurement of how effective one is in a general sense. Even one's IQ has been shown to be affected by mood and perception of well-being.

A child may have a lower IQ than the next person, or slightly less ability. But through greater effort and determination he can close that gap. Effort and determination are fundamentals of achievement.

Two recent studies support this statement. One, by Uni-

180   The Power of Positive Parenting

versity of Denver psychologists Ken Seely and Steven Haravey, found that 10 percent of youths going through a suburban juvenile court system in Denver had superior but *undetected* intelligence. They were properly classified as gifted, a classification that includes only 3 percent of the general population.

Why did their superior intelligence go undetected? Because in school they were underachievers and had not developed the verbal skills on which many IQ tests are based.

A second study, by Illinois educational consultant Roger Taylor, revealed that 17 percent of prisoners serving life sentences in federal penitentiaries have IQ's that would qualify them as gifted. In a related study he found that 19 percent of high school dropouts are in the top 5 percent of the population in intelligence.

The point is clear. No matter how intelligent, when a mind becomes a garbage dump for negative thoughts, when it cannot mentally cull the negative images from the positive, IQ alone is no predictor at all of adult success.

We have talked in this book about attitudes, all kinds of attitudes dealing with self-esteem and interpersonal relations. But there is a single overarching attitude that affects success more than any other—simple *determination*, a willingness never to give up, however difficult the circumstances. Such determination issues from all the other positive attitudes. It comes when a person truly believes that if he can only hang on long enough, success will eventually come. And it might be closer than it seems. Ponder this poem, which offers up some powerful justification for hanging in there!

DON'T QUIT

When things go wrong, as they sometimes will
When the road you're trudging seems all up hill,
When the funds are low and the debts are high,
And when you want to smile, but you have to sigh,
When care is pressing you down a bit,
Rest, if you must—but don't you quit.

Life is queer with its twists and turns,
As every one of us sometimes learns,
And many a failure turns about
When we might have won had we stuck it out;
Don't give up, though the pace seems slow—
You might succeed with another blow.

Often the goal is nearer than
It seems to a faint and faltering man.
Often the struggler has given up
When he might have captured the victor's cup.
And he learned too late, when the night slipped down
How close he was to the golden crown.

Success is failure turned inside out—
The silver tint of the clouds of doubt—
And you never can tell how close you are,
It may be near when it seems afar;
So stick to the fight when you're hardest hit—
It's when things seem worst that you mustn't quit.

Author Unknown

20 Open the Lion's Cage!—Potential for Success

Nothing I have ever accomplished brings me as much pride as knowing that I have taught young people to believe in themselves.

Confucius once said, "The most beautiful sight in the world is a little child going confidently down the road after you have shown him the way." As a parent, and as an educator, I have had the pleasure of seeing that "most beautiful sight," and to me it is the ultimate achievement. Nothing—not doctoral degrees or White House visits or athletic championships—has been as exciting to me as the thrill of awakening young people to their true potential.

Why do I feel so strongly about the importance of positive parents, teachers, and other adults? Because I have seen over and over the impact that such positive persons can make in the lives of young men and women. To me, being a positive influence in their lives is more than just a concept; it is virtually a calling.

Many students have shown me the impact of a single adult's influence, but none has brought it home to me so graphically as a young man named Paul.

Paul was a handsome high school student who played center on the football team I coached years ago in Birmingham. He was a model kid, a hard worker who always had a great attitude, and I became good friends with both him and his parents. I spent many hours in their home during the years he played ball for me.

I left coaching and became a principal. I had moved from Birmingham to Huntsville, about 150 miles away. Then I learned that Paul was gravely ill. He had come home from college during the Christmas holidays, complaining of not feeling well. He went to the doctor, suspecting that he might have mononucleosis.

The diagnosis instead was much worse: acute leukemia, in an advanced state. Paul was told he had a short time to live. As he battled his disease, he constantly astounded the doctors and nurses and friends who visited him; they could hardly believe the courage he showed, the bright, hopeful outlook. People who spent time with him left his hospital room feeling good about *themselves*. They had come to cheer *him*, and left being inspired *by him*.

In the middle of the night, I was awakened at my home by a telephone call from Paul's father. He said Paul had asked to see me, and wondered if I would please drive down to the hospital to talk with him.

"Sure," I told Howard. "First thing in the morning, as soon as I get the kids off to school, I'll drive down there."

"That might be too late, Bill," he responded soberly. "Is it possible you could come tonight?"

Howard would not ask me that, I realized, if things were not very near the end for Paul. I woke Carolyn immediately; we dressed without saying much to each other, went next door to ask our neighbor to stay with the children, and headed south toward Birmingham. We arrived at the hospital before daylight.

We parked the car, got on the elevator, and went straight to the fourth floor. As the elevator doors slid open, Howard was standing in the hallway. "Coach, Paul has been asking to see you; he wants to see you alone."

I went into the hospital room. My first thought was how quickly Paul's condition had deteriorated, how emaciated he looked, how different from the robust young athlete I had coached. I was almost overwhelmed with the sadness of it all. What could I say at a time like this, I wondered, approaching his bed. But before I had time to say anything, Paul reached over the railing of his bed and took my hand.

"Coach," he said weakly, trying to mask sadness with his characteristic smile, "I'm fixin' to cross over the River Jordan. I just didn't want to leave until I told you what you've meant to me."

I swallowed and fought back tears. He continued. "You taught me a lotta things, Coach. You set an example for me. You showed me how to win. And now I realize you showed me how to lose, too—though I'm not so sure I'm losing; I'm not afraid to die.

"Thanks, Coach . . . thanks. For everything. You've been so good for me."

His mother and father came back into the room. He told his mother how much he loved her and then he died.

I left the hospital that night knowing I would never forget that young man and his courage. If something I had done had helped produce the grace and power with which he faced death, it was worth every hour I spent with him on the football field and every conversation we'd ever had. He had shown me that a single adult *can* make a difference, and I left there that night determined that I would never let him down—or any of the thousands of young men and women like him.

There is no greater investment, one offering no higher reward, than that which we give our young people. To face the battles of life, they have only what we teach them. Some will outlive us by many years; some will achieve heights of success we ourselves will never reach; some, like Paul, may have courage and poise tested by the ultimate challenge of early death. We never know. We can only pour ourselves wholeheartedly into the effort of teaching them that they can rise to any challenge that might lie ahead.

OPENING THE LION'S CAGE:
THE AVENUE OF ESCAPE

Developing children with positive mental attitudes offers the opportunity to free the minds and spirits of our youth in much the same way as in the story of the caged lion.

The animal was beautifully developed, muscular, powerful, with a rich coat and proud mane, and deep, gleaming eyes—the very epitome of strength. The unique fact about this lion was that he was housed in a very frail-looking cage. The caretaker of the zoo was often questioned by visitors: "Is that cage really as fragile as it looks?"

"Yes, it actually is not a strong cage at all," the caretaker explained.

"Then why on earth doesn't the lion escape?" visitors always asked. And the caretaker explained: "Well, you see, when this lion was caged, he was just a cub, not strong enough to break these bars. Somewhere during these many months that have passed, the lion crossed over that invisible line, from being unable to break the bars to being *able* to break them. But because he is unaware of his power, he has no confidence in himself, and he therefore doesn't even try to escape."

When I consider our homes and schools today, I think of all the caged minds they hold. They are not only the minds of underprivileged or poverty-stricken students, but the minds of a large majority of the entire student population, students from all socioeconomic levels. Their minds are locked in four-walled cubicles of self-doubt, poor self-image, visions of fears and failures, and lack of self-confidence. Those four walls can form an awesome barrier for a young person who has never tested the strength that lies inherently within, who has never been inspired to break down the barriers.

Children are hampered not so much by lack of financial substance and proper social background or by environmental restraints as by the creeping paralysis of the mind that reflects our negative society. They have been overexposed to such statements as "You can't afford that," "I can't see you as college material," "You aren't capable of going very far," "You're just a loser," "Better not try that or you'll fail"—and they grow up, like the lion cub, with their strong, youthful bodies and minds wasting away in a cage.

The past several years have seen the development and implementation of a unique program in thousands of America's schools and homes. The *Power of Positive Students* program has accomplished one very significant feat: it has brought into focus the indisputable truth that there is a measurable correlation between mental attitude and personal achievement!

In homes and schools across the nation, parents and teachers have the power to open the lion's cage. It is the simple power of positive parenting, teaching, and modeling a positive lifestyle, showing young people that their limits are self-imposed, that they can break out into successful and productive behavior.

God did not intend that lions live in cages. He created them with particular instincts and abilities and placed them in a habitat in which they could utilize those natural characteristics.

God gifted humans similarly. He gave each of us an *intellect*—a power that can shrivel in captivity or grow strong in freedom.

As a parent you have a dual responsibility: to offer your youngster mental freedom and to prepare him to accept that freedom *positively*. Your youngster's mind is among the millions capable of great achievement or dismal failure. It can someday *cure* social ills or add to them; it can provide leadership in any field from science and government to the arts and humanities. Or it can wallow in mediocrity.

So much depends on you. I urge you to unlock the cage, tear down the bars, and transform it into a theater-in-the-round! Use that theater as a stage for daily guidance—where your words, your actions, your expressions, your every form of communication with your youngster, is motivationally positive.

Success and happiness are available to every child, bar none.

So! LET'S OPEN THAT LION'S CAGE . . . so that an in-